America's Rivalry
THE 20 GREATEST REDSKINS-COWBOYS GAMES

By Mickey Spagnola, John Keim,
David Elfin and Rick Snider

ISBN: 0-9656057-1-X

For additional copies, call 1-800-408-8379

To Dominick and Grace, the best and most supportive parents a kid possessed by some silly dream of becoming a sports writer could ever have, and my wife Gail, who still puts up with this nonsense.

— Mickey Spagnola

To my mom and friend, Lou, who showered us as kids with her most valuable asset — time — and continues to sacrifice for us. And to my grandmother, Josephine Ulle, the sweetest person I know.

— John Keim

To my mother, Margery, who taught me a very important reporter's tool: how to listen.
— David Elfin

To my late father, William Snider, who continues to inspire me, and my mother, Margy, for her continued support.

— Rick Snider

Thanks to . . .

The authors would like to thank Progressive Publishing Group, Inc., graphic designer Patricia Nieves, Arnie Sachs and Consolidated News Photo, Dick Burke for supplying photos from his late father Ranny Routt's collection, the public relations staffs of the Washington Redskins and Dallas Cowboys, Redskins owner John Kent Cooke, Sr., Cowboys owner Jerry Jones and vice president George Hays, Janie Tilford, Mary Barnes, Erin Anthony, Jim Foster and Frank Luksa, Washington Times sports editor Gary Hopkins and Journal sports editor Paul Bergeron for their contributions and support of the book. We also offer a very special thanks to former Cowboys president, and Hall of Famer, Tex Schramm, a man who understands the significance of preserving history. Also, thanks to artist Terry Crews for the book's cover illustration.

Table of Contents

Redskins Victories:

Cowboys Victories:

All-Time Rivalry Team
DALLAS COWBOYS
Offense

QUARTERBACK .... Roger Staubach

RUNNING BACKS .... Tony Dorsett, Emmitt Smith

CENTER .... Mark Stepnoski

GUARDS .... John Niland, Nate Newton

TACKLES .... Rayfield Wright, Mark Tuinei

TIGHT END .... Billy Joe DuPree

RECEIVERS .... Drew Pearson, Michael Irvin

Defense

ENDS ....Harvey Martin, Ed (Too Tall) Jones

TACKLES .... Randy White, Bob Lilly

LINEBACKERS .... Lee Roy Jordan, Chuck Howley, Dave Edwards

SAFETIES .... Cliff Harris, Darren Woodson

CORNERBACKS .... Mel Renfro, Everson Walls

Special Teams

KICKER..Rafael Septien

PUNTER .... Danny White

RETURNER...Bob Hayes

PLAYER .... Bill Bates

COACH .... Tom Landry

All-Time Rivalry Team
WASHINGTON REDSKINS
Offense

QUARTERBACK .... Sonny Jurgensen

RUNNING BACKS .... Larry Brown, John Riggins

CENTER .... Len Hauss

GUARDS .... Mark May, Russ Grimm

TACKLES .... Jim Lachey, Joe Jacoby

TIGHT END.. Jerry Smith

RECEIVERS .... Charley Taylor, Art Monk

Defense

ENDS .... Dexter Manley, Charles Mann

TACKLES .... Diron Talbert, Dave Butz

LINEBACKERS .... Ken Harvey, Chris Hanburger, Neal Olkewicz

SAFETIES .... Brig Owens, Ken Houston

CORNERBACKS .... Darrell Green, Pat Fischer

Special Teams

KICKER... Mark Moseley

PUNTER .... Mike Bragg

RETURNER .... Mike Nelms

PLAYER .... Bill Malinchak

COACH .... George Allen

photo by Joe Silverman/The Washington Times

Dallas' Roger Staubach and Washington's Diron Talbert shared the rivalry's spotlight in the 1970s, for their actions and their words.

Bitter Rivals, Sweet Memories

There had to be a beginning to all this bitterness, the down-right hatred and the below-the-belt skullduggery grown men from both sides have engaged in to create this Cowboys-Redskins thing, this rivalry waged now for 37 years between not only two National Football League teams, but between two cities, and really, when you get right down to it, two ways of life.

Most rivalries are a natural. If there is an Army, there is certain to be antagonism with a Navy. If there is a college in Ohio, that one in Michigan is unlikely to be real neighborly. If there are two baseball teams in one city, allegiance becomes nearly genetic: You're a Cubs fan or a White Sox fan, unable to even mildly tolerate the other. If there is a North, then the ready-made opposite is the South. Same with cats and dogs, man and woman, Hatfields and McCoys.

But Dallas Cowboys and Washington Redskins?

The cities were worlds apart. The teams had little in common, the Redskins NFL old-guard and the Cowboys nouveau riche. And the players had little reason at the start to feud. The Redskins had been so bad and the Cowboys were so bad that jealousy would have been hard-pressed to even be petty.

So where lies the genesis for the antagonistic relationship these two real, American rivals have shared since 1960, when the Redskins were 28-years old and the Cowboys were entering their inaugural NFL season? After all, what has taken place ever since is outer limits.

American presidents have offered advice to coaches. Coaches have sent telegrams to presidents. A president circling in Air Force One once called to congratulate a Saudi prince on his favorite team's victory. Players have sent telegrams to newspapers. Fans have sent funeral wreaths to teams. Hotels have been bought out for security reasons. Hot water has been turned off in showers. Arms have been broken. Knees have been cracked. Scars have been born. Heads have bobbed. Signals jammed. Wreaths thrown. Trash dumped. A bottle cracked on the head of a player's mom. Fingers raised.

There have been fights, lots of fights. Songs have been sung. Words have been slung. Spies have been spotted. Gag orders issued. Feelings rubbed raw and victories rubbed in. And even when the participants in this 100-yard drama move on to another life, they have a hard time forgetting what once was.

"When you sign with Washington, you sign a contract to hate the Cowboys," said Charles Mann, an 11-year Washington veteran of these Cowboys-Redskins battles, the last in 1993.

The Cowboys certainly understood that. If they didn't, the RFK faithful made sure they did.

"The fans in RFK hated the Cowboys," Cowboys free safety Cliff Harris said. "There were only 55,000 of them, but it was such a closed stadium, the sound reverberated. I've often said if they would have let the gates down, and said it was OK to kill the Cowboys, the fans would have killed the Cowboys.

"They'd just kill you on the field."

Those intense feelings the participants felt may subside when playing days are over, but they never die. Not even time is potent enough stain-remover for this deeply ingrained bitterness the two sides have passed on from generation to generation.

"About six or seven years ago we played this old-timers flag football game in RFK," remembered Cowboys receiver Drew Pearson, who last faced the Redskins in 1983. "We shared the same locker room, Cowboys and Redskins. Just wanted to have fun. We had a great dinner and fellowship together the night before, and then here we are in the third quarter and Pat Fischer and I are going at it again."

That's right, Fischer, the little Redskins cornerback Pearson to this day considers the third best he faced, behind only Pittsburgh's Mel Blount and the Cowboys' Mel Renfro.

"He cold-cocks me one time, and I get up and retaliate," said Pearson, reiterating that this was *flag* football. "And he says, 'You're not serious, are you?' I say, 'Hell yes I'm serious. I'll take your head off.'"

Boys will be boys and men still will be boys when the Cowboys and Redskins are involved.

And maybe that is exactly why all this began, men still trying to be boys in the 1960s, a turbulent period of U. S. history when Vietnam, assassinations, the space race, the Cuban missile crisis, riots, campus unrest, the Bay of Pigs and the civil rights struggle created high tension and an even higher need for escape.

Because in 1960, along comes this little bespectacled Texan named Clint Murchison Jr., with beaucoup money, and who wants nothing more than to own an NFL team in Dallas. And with typical

7

Texan impatience, he wanted to start now.

But legendary Washington owner George Preston Marshall balked. Murchison needed Marshall's vote to gain acceptance into the NFL.

"But for some reason he wanted us to start a year later, and wanted to make sure we were in his division," said Tex Schramm, the Cowboys' president during their first 29 seasons and Murchison's right-hand.

The devilish Murchison knew how to swing a deal. You get one up first. And little did Marshall know, but Murchison had bought the rights to "Hail to the Redskins," played mightily at all Washington home games by the Redskins Band. "And that was like the Star Spangled Banner to George Preston," Schramm said. "They started all their games – he was the only one that had a real marching band – by first playing Dixie and then Hail to the Redskins."

So Murchison, the little big man, mentioned to Marshall just who owned the rights to "Hail to the Redskins." Then added, if Marshall did not approve of Dallas receiving a franchise he just couldn't see how it would be possible for Washington to continue playing "his" song.

The Cowboys got their vote, "and Clint gave George Preston his song," Schramm said.

Then Texas got its vote, the election of President John F. Kennedy in 1960 turned Texas' Democratic senator, Lyndon Baines Johnson, into Vice President and then the President following Kennedy's assassination in 1963. After that, even more of those independent-minded, strong-willed Texans came to Washington to run the government.

"Just so many Texans up there because of politics," said Tom Landry, the Cowboys' coach for their first 29 years. "We had such a great following there."

Thus the birth of what became known as the Cowboys Chicken Club (CCC), a bunch of Murchison cronies who were Washington high-rollers with too much money and evidently, too much time on their hands.

"Clint was the ultimate practical joker," Schramm said. "There was no end he wouldn't go to do something."

Murchison had his boys in Washington. Guys such as Tom Webb, Irv Davidson, Bob Thompson and Francis "Reds" Bagnell. They were lobbyists and what-nots. Or as Schramm called them, "Real men's men," guys who thought nothing of putting a man's yacht in his backyard swimming pool on his birthday or buying some guy a road grader and parking the contraption on his front lawn.

Well, the boys decided to pester Marshall in his new D.C Stadium. Marshall always planned elaborate halftime shows, and on Dec. 17, 1961, the Redskins' owner was putting on his annual Christmas extravaganza, complete with Santa Claus being pulled onto the field in a dog-drawn sleigh. What better laugh could there be than to disrupt the halftime show, maybe even knock Santa off his perch.

So Thompson and the boys snuck 50 chickens, packed in wooden crates, into the stadium, hiding them in the baseball dugout nearest the Dallas bench. Then they sowed the field with chicken feed at night, figuring to turn the chickens loose when Santa arrived and watch them create holy terror feasting on the seed all over the field.

"The plan was that the dogs would see the chickens and away we'd go," Schramm laughs to this day.

Amazingly, with halftime mere minutes away, no one had detected these chickens stashed in the dugout. No one had even heard all the clucking. That is, until this guy came walking by, doing a double-take when he heard what he thought were chickens clucking in the middle of a football stadium with an NFL game in progress.

And as Bud Shrake of the Dallas Morning News wrote, the guy asked the man Shrake appropriately named the Cowboys Chicken Club *agent*, who had been guarding these chickens all along and who was responsible for their release, "What's in there?"

"Ice cream," the agent said.

The CCC agent thought the guy was an usher, and tried to bribe him with a $100 bill to go away. He should have been so lucky. The guy just happened to be Dick McCann, Washington's general manager. The police were called. The CCC agent and the chickens were sent to jail, the halftime show saved.

Of course, the Cowboys disclaimed knowledge of any such shenanigans when Marshall vehemently complained to the league.

The CCC wasn't finished. The next year during what was becoming known as Cowboys Week in Washington, the boys began making prank phone calls to Marshall, who would answer his private line only to hear chickens clucking on the other end. Marshall complained to NFL Commissioner Pete Rozelle, who not only warned the Cowboys, but also Davidson and Thompson at a party the night before the Nov. 4 game.

That same night, though, the Redskins' faithful struck back. When Thompson went back to his hotel suite after the party, there to greet him as he opened the bathroom door was a 43-pound turkey with a Cowboys sticker stuck to its chest.

"All I know is we brought something home on the plane after that game, something that would bite the hell out of you," Schramm said.

Touche, thought the CCC. So as the Redskins Band marched onto the field playing "Hail to the Redskins" this Nov. 4, 1962, Sunday afternoon, four banners unraveled from the rim of the upper deck, complete with the words "chickens." Then two guys dressed in chicken costumes jumped from the stands and began weaving through the band. From a sack, they littered the field with colored eggs as security guards chased closely behind. One of the "chickens" even threw out a live chicken as the band was playing the National Anthem.

"So when you start talking about a rivalry," Schramm said, "we started off with a real heated rivalry."

Especially after the Cowboys won that game, 38-10, registering their first win over Washington, and Cowboys quarterback Eddie LeBaron — an ex-Redskin — becoming the first Dallas player to duck a whiskey bottle heaved in his direction by an irate Washington fan. But certainly not the last.

Forever more, Cowboys and Redskins had become real life Cowboys and Indians. And as the Cowboys improved, going to the NFL championship games in 1966 and 1967, the Redskins struggled, at one point from 1968-70 losing six consecutive games to those uppity guys from Dallas.

"But George Allen was responsible for igniting the rivalry that was growing," Schramm said of the former Los Angeles Rams coach taking over the Redskins in 1971.

If there is any truism to this rivalry, that is. Allen fueled all. As the normally mild-mannered Cowboys Hall of Fame cornerback Mel Renfro is wont to say, "He was basically a crook. The Richard Nixon of football."

Be it "Skins-Gate" or not, Allen brought winning football back to the nation's capital. He brought in old, experienced players – the "Over The Hill Gang" – to challenge the Cowboys for supremacy in the NFC East. In fact, Allen's Redskins beat the Cowboys the first time they met in 1971. The next year, Washington won the division, and whipped Dallas in the NFC Championship Game to reach its first Super Bowl.

"George understood when he came to Washington, that if the Redskins were to be any good, they

photo by Kevin Gilbert/The Washington Times

Cowboys receiver Michael Irvin and Redskins cornerback Darrell Green have long had a rivalry.

had to consistently beat the Cowboys," said Calvin Hill, a rivalry turncoat of sorts, having played six years for the Cowboys (1969-74) and two years for the Redskins (1976-77). "Once he went to Washington, the Cowboys were the enemy.

"Suddenly it became Dallas and Washington, and it caught the imagination of so many people, not only because it was Cowboys and Indians, but the lure of how we romanticized that part of our history. The Western expansion. It was Dallas versus Washington, a Sunbelt city, gleaming, sort of neo-traditional architecture, Southwest, versus the sophisticated East, the center of power.

"But then one of the great ambiguities to me was the team from the sort of rough-and-tough city, the oil city, was a sophisticated football team – textbook, computers and all that. And the team that represented the establishment city, the center of power, was a rough-and-tough team. It was almost a reversal. I mean Washington was federal government, bastion of regulations, and here you had laissez-faire Dallas, damn the regulations and damn the regulators."

The cities, the teams, the players – even the coaches – had become the other's antithesis.

Immediately the Cowboys became paranoid about Allen rooms during Redskins Week. Later they would ask the hotel manager not to rent those rooms during those weeks.

And even that was not being careful enough when dealing with Allen. The Cowboys actually moved their practices, sometimes to a high school stadium, sometimes into the Cotton Bowl, just to make sure security was at its highest.

"When I came down here, I figured football was football," said running back Preston Pearson, who played two years in Baltimore (1968-69) and five years in Pittsburgh (1970-74) before his 1975 arrival in Dallas. "But I found out there was no better rivalry than Dallas and Washington. And the week of the game there was no comparison. The coaches got harder on you. They got tight. Everybody was watching.

"I mean Landry had people walking behind the fence at the hotel, checking things out. When I first got here and saw that, I asked [guard] Blaine Nye, 'What are they doing over there? What are guys doing at the hotel over there looking in the windows?' And guys explained to me, 'Hey, this is Redskins Week. Things get tight around here. They don't allow certain things to happen. They don't allow people in the locker room.' They were checking things out with binoculars. It was like, wow, what the hell is going on around here?

"But once you're in it, you're in it. You become part of it."

No amount of caution was too much once Allen arrived. The Cowboys actually traced a suspicious car parked at one of their practices to a Dallas airport rental agency, rented in the name of a Redskins scout.

"Any helicopter that came over," said Cowboys fullback Walt Garrison, "the coaches would look up like, 'Damn, that's George Allen up there with a notebook.'"

Allen also was a tad paranoid, hiring a security agent to patrol his practices, having once accused Cowboys scout Bucko Kilroy of climbing a tree to spy on his Rams practices. "Bucko was 300 pounds," Landry said with a laugh.

Allen stopped at nothing to cause consternation in Dallas.

"George used to call Tom Landry during the week of the game and ask how his team was," said Washington defensive tackle Diron Talbert, one of Allen's favorite conduits for instigation. "Landry would have to be thinking, 'That goofy SOB, what's he calling me for?' We'd be sitting in a jacuzzi and he'd come in

and get in a crouched position and say, 'We're gonna get that Staubach and ring his neck!'"

Oh, the many stories these two teams have provided.

The Redskins accused Cowboys wide receiver Lance Alworth in 1972 of trying to purposely hurt the knee of linebacker Jack Pardee with a crack-back block, and then Redskins wide receiver Charley Taylor getting even with the Cowboys, blowing out linebacker Chuck Howley's knee with a similar block. Pardee missed a quarter, Howley the rest of the season.

There was Dallas punt snapper D.D. Lewis' infamous head-bob, drawing the Redskins offside in 1977, the penalty yardage allowing the Cowboys to continue driving down field for the winning score. There were the end-of-the-game fights, mostly provoked by Washington quarterback Joe Theismann, first by mocking the Cowboys while taking a game-ending safety in 1978 and later by trying to run out the clock in 1984.

And it seems each participant has his own special memory.

For Washington wide receiver Charley Taylor, born and raised in Grand Prairie, Texas, a suburb of Dallas, his was living in the wrong city – or playing for the wrong team.

"That game I blocked Chuck Howley, and it was a legal block, for the next couple of months my mom had threatening phone calls," said Taylor (1964-77), a Hall of Famer. "I can't repeat what they said to her, but it wasn't pretty. I had brothers and sisters in school, and they were being taunted."

For Cowboys free safety Cliff Harris, it was always the cold showers at RFK. Harris was convinced Allen ordered the stadium crew to turn off the hot water in the Cowboys' locker room.

"The locker rooms are dank and dark and musty, and the one thing an athlete looks for after a game or competition is a warm shower," Harris said. "And typically, it would start to snow at the end of the game there. It was real cold, you were beat up, and you were covered with green [paint from the grass] and the black stuff under your eyes. And what would happen is George Allen would have turned the hot water off.

"So you're beaten up, you go in the shower to wash off, you're freezing to death, you want a hot shower and it's a *cold* shower. So you try your best to wash the green off and the black stuff, but your hair is still matted. And you fly back to Dallas on the charter covered in green, with dark smudges still under your eyes and your hair still has grass in it and you had your tail beaten. Man, even the fans had thrown stuff on you on the way out.

"Ahhh, it was great. I used to love it."

Remembered Cowboys defensive end Harvey Martin, "I mean nothing but cold water. Damn Redskins. And *you know* they've got hot water. You know they're showering good."

The Cowboys' charges are justified. Washington quarterback Billy Kilmer said the man in charge of the water was Redskins equipment manager Tom McVean.

"George told Tom to turn off the hot water so Dallas would have a cold shower," Kilmer said.

Martin, the center of controversy with Washington most of his career, never will forget the 1982 game at RFK after he filed for bankruptcy in Dallas, maybe more so than the time he slung a funeral wreath sent to the Cowboys' practice facility into the Redskins' locker room following Dallas quarterback Roger Staubach's memorable comeback victory in the crucial 1979 finale.

"We fly to Washington, and I don't hear anything [about the bankruptcy], so I figure, like OK," Martin said. "Then I'm going on the field, coming out of that little dugout, and I hear this 'bing, bing, bing.' Something is bouncing off my helmet. Then I turn around, and the fans are screaming, 'Hey Harvey, want a loooaaaannn?' They are throwing pennies and stuff at my helmet. Throwing nickels at me, man. The fans are throwing change."

As if it wasn't bad enough, Redskins defensive end Dexter Manley continued the needling right in the middle of the game. "We're getting ready to kick an extra point, and Dexter gets up, looks at me and says, 'Hey Harvey, you need any extra money, maaaannnnn,' " said Martin, who also remembered the time he was fined $3,000 for knocking Theismann out of a game with a deliberate and accurate right cross.

The intensity of this hatred for one another carried into the 1980s. Quarterback Babe Laufenberg, who began his career with Washington as a rookie out of Indiana in 1983 and ended his career with a season-ending start and loss as a Cowboys in 1990, never will forget his NFL baptism, Sept. 5, 1983, a Monday nighter in RFK Stadium, Cowboys and Redskins.

"We got on the sidelines, and everyone is jacked up," said Laufenberg, raised to near cult-figure by

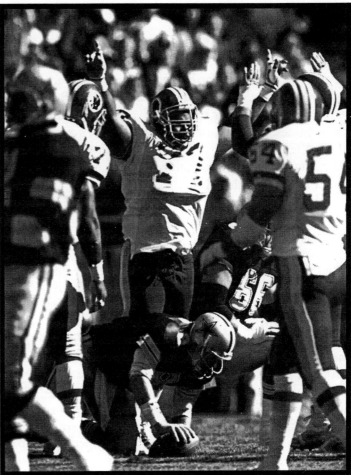

photo courtesy of the Washington Redskins

A sacked Dallas quarterback is always reason to celebrate in Washington.

the Washington fans. "I'm standing next to [offensive line coach] Joe Bugel. Joe was all worked up – chomping at the bit – acting as if he was getting ready to play himself. Then he looks across the field, and he just starts screaming, 'Stautner, Stautner, I'm going to kick your ass …' "

This was Stautner, as in Dallas defensive coordinator Ernie Stautner, a Hall of Fame defensive lineman with the Pittsburgh Steelers who even at his advanced age had a barrel chest and tree-trunk arms. And this rivalry between the two coordinators was nothing new, Bugel having been seen flipping off Stautner before the 1982 NFC Championship Game.

"So I just assumed, being a rookie, that's the way it goes around here," Laufenberg said. "So I start to holler, 'Yeah, Stautner, I'm going to kick …' Then I turn to the guy next to me and ask, 'Who's Stautner?' He tells me it's the guy in the blue shirt on the 40, and I see this guy with arms like fire hydrants, so I turn and yell, 'Landry … Landry, I'm going to kick *your* ass.' And the funny thing about all this when I look back, it was so loud you couldn't hear from you to me, let alone across the field."

But no matter the tales, no matter what side tells them, this rivalry always seems to return to Allen, the man who left the Redskins after seven seasons and who actually was hired by Schramm in 1988 to be the color analyst for the Cowboys' televised pre-season games. The hire just about blew Landry's mind when Allen strolled onto Dallas' Thousand Oaks, Calif., practice facility, Schramm recalled Landry saying, "I never thought I'd see this day."

Allen hated everything about Dallas. The Redskins had a young defensive end named Dallas Hickman.

Allen refused to call him by his first name. Detested the name. "He would call me Dulles or Berkeley," said Hickman, a California-Berkeley graduate, of the family name given him that Allen avoided using at all costs.

Schramm insisted Allen placed banners at RFK, and remembered one reading, "Schramm: Rozelle can't save you now." Understand, the Redskins were thoroughly convinced Schramm and NFL Commissioner Pete Rozelle were in cahoots to give the Cowboys every advantage possible. Especially since Schramm was a mainstay on the NFL's Competition Committee.

Hill, though, will never forget Allen's Cowboys Week antics when he arrived in Washington after a year's stay in the World Football League. Like the time he showed up for practice dragging this laundry bag all around the field. Hill says, "Allen goes, 'I know you want to know what's in this bag. It's Tom Landry in the bag. I'm going to drag him around all day like we will on Sunday.'"

Or the time Allen gave a little karate demonstration to The Gang.

"He comes in with this Kung Fu smock on, and he has three Asians behind him carrying these blocks of wood," said Hill, one of the Asians being karate master Jhoon Rhee. "Then he says, 'I wish it was me and Tom Landry at the 50-yard line Sunday,' and he gives this blood-curdling yell, one guy holds up the block of wood, he hits it with his fist, and it breaks. Then he does it again, breaks another. But the third one, it doesn't break. George just walks out without saying a thing."

This all may have been an act, but Allen's time spent in Los Angeles with the Rams must have paid off. He was a darn convincing actor.

"George wouldn't use the word Dallas," said current Washington general manager Charley Casserly, who began his Redskins career when Allen brought

in the former high school teacher/coach for a non-paying internship in 1977. "He would call them the 'damn Cowboys.' If you lost to Dallas, it was like the end of the world.

"He made it special. He made it personal."

But no matter what happened back then, and for some of the participants it's been twentysomething years, when you talk Cowboys-Redskins these days the blood still boils. And for good reason. This series has defined careers, ruined careers; defined seasons, ruined seasons.

Just consider these curious circumstances: Landry's last victory was over the Redskins. Richie Petitbon's first victory as Washington's coach was over Dallas. Staubach's last regular-season victory was against the Redskins. Vince Lombardi finished his only year as Washington's coach (1969) with a game against the Cowboys before dying nine months later. The Cowboys' only victory in 1989 was against the Redskins. Washington's only regular-season loss during that 1982 strike season was to Dallas, but the Redskins later would clinch their first NFC title in 10 years with a victory over the Cowboys. Washington Hall of Fame running back John Riggins' final game (1979) before his walkout in 1980 was a loss to the Cowboys. Washington's first loss in 1991, having gone 11-0, was to the Cowboys. Theismann's last complete regular season game was against Dallas. Washington coach Norv Turner, the former Dallas offensive coordinator, clinched his first winning season with a victory over the Cowboys. And how fitting that the last game the Redskins played at 36-year-old RFK Stadium was against the Cowboys.

"You just despised that team," said Washington offensive tackle Joe Jacoby (1981-93). "It was genuine. Such a perfect thing – Cowboys and Indians. I still despise the team, even more now because they are so flamboyant."

Jacoby is not alone.

"Because of my position I'm not supposed to think that way," said TNT analyst Mark May, a Redskins guard from 1981-89, when asked if he still hates the Cowboys. "But in the back of my mind, and in my heart, I never like to see them win. It's just inbred in my blood since I was a Redskin. I bleed burgundy and gold. I will always have that in my soul to hate the silver and blue."

As far as Redskins offensive tackle Jim Lachey [1988-94] is concerned, the same goes with the fans.

"If you grow up in metro Washington, you grow up a diehard Redskins fan," he said. "But if you hate your parents, you grow up a Cowboys fan."

This just seems to get in your blood. And for

some, such as Martin, the rivalry haunted his soul. To this day he remembers that January day in 1986, some two years after retiring from the game, when all the Super Bowl MVPs were invited to New Orleans for a halftime parade during Super Bowl XX. That meant Redskins were in his presence, including Riggins.

"And I just couldn't stand him," Martin said. "The man had done nothing to me. Nothing. But the minute he walked onto the field, I got pissed off, and I stayed that way the whole time. And thank God I've stopped drinking and doing drugs, because that night I was drinking a lot, and I was getting more and more worked up just looking at him. Seriously. I just hated him, and I hated the Redskins."

Martin left the game early, walking back to his hotel room and leaving his girlfriend behind. Alone, she just happened to latch on to Riggins and his group of friends.

"I found out, and threw her out of the room – because she was with John Riggins' friends," Martin said. "I think I've changed since, but the hatred went that deep."

So deep, being out of work was far more palatable than playing for the Redskins. Cowboys cornerback Ron Fellows said Washington called after Dallas didn't re-sign him in 1987. "I didn't even bother taking the trip," said Fellows, responsible for igniting a game-ending brawl. "I didn't like them. It would be like real Indians putting on a cowboys [outfit] and going out and fighting the Indians. That doesn't make any sense, trying to get an Apache scalp. It would be like, 'Hey, what are you fighting us for?' It wasn't anything personal with the players. I just didn't like them."

But of all the Cowboys, the Redskins' rivalry seemed to define the career of Charlie Waters (1970-81), who lost a starting cornerback job because of his play in a Redskins game; who broke his arm trying to return a punt against the Redskins; who broke in as a radio analyst while injured for a Redskins game; and who jumped into the stands with teammate Randy White to pummel the fan that had cracked a beer bottle over his helmet after a Redskins game.

To this day, every day of his life Waters remembers the Redskins.

photo by Arnie Sachs/Consolidated News Pictures

The Cowboys' defense pursued Redskins quarterback Joe Theismann with extra vigor.

"I should have gone to the last game at RFK," Waters said of the 1996 season finale against the Cowboys. "It was just a wonderful, hate, hate, hate relationship. All those stupid things we said about each other prior to the game. They'd say mean things. Harvey throws a wreath at them. It was wonderful, wonderful stuff.

"And I've got this huge scar on my face to this day. Charley Taylor kicked me in the mouth, and I've got this L-shaped scar in front of my face and jaw. I got 30 stitches, and because they stitched me on the field so I could finish the game, it left a real, nice, little scar. Every day I looked in the mirror I'd be pissed off at Charley Taylor and the Redskins.

"It's forever."

The memories. The hard feelings. The laughs. The sorrows. They too are forever, as everlasting as America's Rivalry — Cowboys-Redskins — self-conceived, self-sustained, these fictional-like characters its heart and soul.

photo by Arnie Sachs/Consolidated News Pictures

No Dallas lead was safe with Sonny Jurgensen throwing passes for Washington.

Nov. 28, 1965

Classic Comeback

Redskins 34, Cowboys 31

One by one they arrived in Washington, stung either by their departure from another city or by their failure to land somewhere else — like Dallas. Together the trio embarked on Hall of Fame careers.

First, though, they had to recover from this stigma: They were Redskins. In the early 1960s, that wasn't a desired identification.

So Sonny Jurgensen sat stunned in a Philadelphia delicatessen; Bobby Mitchell was bewildered in Cleveland and Charley Taylor cried in Texas.

They joined an organization that had just three winning seasons between 1946 and 1961. In those last two years, the Redskins won two games. They lost 21.

Welcome to Washington. Hail to the Redskins.

First came Mitchell in 1962, brought to Washington for one purpose — integration. His path to Washington was paved by Secretary of the Interior Stewart Udall, who threatened to evict the Redskins from their new federally-owned stadium unless they added a black player. Washington, which held the No. 1 pick in the 1962 draft, traded with perennial contender Cleveland for the established star.

Oddly, the deal was struck during the 1961 season, but Mitchell finished off the year with the Browns. He never learned of the trade until after the season, but teammate Jim Brown knew and late in the year told Mitchell he was sorry for what was happening. Mitchell had no clue what he was talking about.

When Mitchell played against Washington in past seasons, he would notice a large percentage of black people in town and thought whoever integrated the team would be lucky. He was wrong.

"My first two years, if I could throw them out somewhere, I'd be giving away All-Pro years, but I'd give them away anyway," Mitchell said. "I came here as a star and that was too much for people. It was pretty tough for the whites and it was very tough for me with the blacks because they wanted me to be a superstar every game. I couldn't drop a ball; I couldn't fumble and I didn't have the luxury of saying, 'I'm sorry.'"

Taylor and Jurgensen arrived next. Taylor came via the draft, but the Grand Prairie, Texas native had his heart set on playing for the Cowboys. Dallas, which joined the league in 1960, had begun to accumulate a wealth of talent such as quarterback Don Meredith, defensive tackle Bob Lilly, running back Don Perkins and linebacker Lee Roy Jordan. Taylor wanted to be part of this group.

But the Redskins won a coin flip with the Cowboys for the first pick. They selected Taylor, a running back from Arizona State.

"When one of my college teammates heard it on the radio and told me, I actually laid back on my bed and cried," Taylor said.

Then the Redskins obtained Jurgensen in the spring of 1964, about an hour after he met with new Philadelphia coach Joe Kuharich. No trade had been discussed. Jurgensen was eating lunch at a delicatessen when someone informed him of the deal after it was broadcast on the radio.

It was April Fool's Day. But this was no joke.

"I was shocked," said Jurgensen, who had thrown 64 touchdown passes the previous three seasons.

But he would eventually echo what Taylor and Mitchell said.

"It was the best thing that ever happened to me," Jurgensen said.

And the three of them were the best things that happened to Washington in the 1960s. That was never more true than on Nov. 28, 1965 at D.C. Stadium in a matchup of disappointing teams. Though the Cowboys, who had added speedy rookies Bob Hayes at receiver and Dan Reeves at running back, opened the season with two straight wins, they lost their next five and entered with a 4-6 record, same as the Redskins.

Washington, shut out of the playoffs since 1945, had high hopes after a 6-8 finish the previous season, its first with the high-powered passing attack in place. But the Redskins lost their first five games in 1965, the offense scoring just 47 points. Jurgensen was even benched during that stretch against St. Louis in favor of Dick Shiner, a local favorite who had starred at Maryland. Washington lost, 37-16. The problem wasn't Jurgensen.

But the Redskins escaped this muck. They won four of the next five, averaging 25.3 points a game in the victories. This matchup, however, produced mostly yawns in the nation's capital as The Washington Star devoted just 10 paragraphs to the preview story the day of the game.

The game was anything but a yawner as the Redskins dug out of a 21-0 hole, completing the best comeback in team history. Jurgensen, Taylor and Mitchell led the rally. But they also contributed to the first-half troubles, especially Jurgensen and Taylor.

Lilly returned a first-quarter Jurgensen fumble 41 yards to the Washington 6, setting up a 6-yard Meredith touchdown pass to running back Perry Lee Dunn; Taylor fumbled — on third-and-33 from the Redskins' 2 — and safety Cornell Green returned the ball for a touchdown and 14-0 lead.

Washington then recovered a fumble and moved into field goal range. More trouble followed as Mike Gaechter blocked Bob Jencks' kick and returned the loose ball 60 yards for a 21-0 lead.

"I just turned on my Bob Hayes speed," said Gaechter, a safety.

Here's how the Redskins responded on their next series: Taylor dropped a pass; Jurgensen overthrew Mitchell; Jurgensen was sacked for a loss of seven and, on fourth down, Pat Richter punted the ball just 26 yards.

"I think that's about the worst series of downs I've ever seen, pro, college or high school," Jurgensen said. "[But] during all that time we were stinking the place out, we never lost our poise."

Taylor and Jurgensen connected on a 26-yard touchdown pass to salvage something from the first half. But the extra point was blocked and Dallas led, 21-6, at halftime.

That late score, however, provided little comfort to the 50,205 fans in attendance. They booed Jurgensen loudly in the first half, chanting for Shiner. The boos got so loud, Jurgensen said he nearly stuck up his hand, asking for quiet so his teammates could hear his signals.

"Imagine what they would have thought then," Jurgensen said after the game, "that I was trying to get them to stop asking for Dick."

Jurgensen had completed just 9-of-20 passes for 108 yards. His first pass was blocked, his second was intercepted. On the next series he fumbled. And on the third series, Taylor, who would be switched to receiver in 1966, fumbled.

Mitchell, shifted to receiver after the trade, caught two passes for just 17 yards.

But Dallas had witnessed Jurgensen explosions before. In a November 1961 game, Eagles fans booed Jurgensen from the start. Their anger increased when Jurgensen's first two passes were intercepted. A good friend later admitted to Jurgensen that he, too, had booed.

Jurgensen finished the game with five touchdown passes.

That's why Dallas coach Tom Landry didn't feel safe against the Redskins, despite a 15-point advantage. Besides, his offense had done zilch, gaining just 95 yards. Washington had sacked Meredith twice and intercepted him once. The Cowboys also had lost a fumble.

"It's like a fighter who has his man on the ropes then steps back to let him rest up," Landry said. "We should have put them away in the first half, but the offense couldn't get going."

Credit a Redskins defense led by safety Paul Krause, who picked off Meredith, and linebacker Sam Huff, who recovered a fumble. This was an emotional game for Huff, whose 35-year-old brother, Donald, had died three days earlier of a heart attack. Huff drove to Washington from Farmington, W.Va., the day of the game and returned immediately afterward for the Monday funeral.

That's a heavy enough burden without what the offense was asking the defense to do. Midway through the third quarter, a Taylor fumble returned the ball to Dallas at the Washington 42. Danny Villanueva's 30-yard field goal boosted the lead to 24-6.

Jurgensen then seized control. He directed a 90-yard drive, completing three passes for 57 yards and punctuating it with a 1-yard sneak.

"Once Sonny turned it loose, it just mushroomed," said Mitchell, who caught one of those passes for 22 yards. "We felt we were the best passing team in football and that sometime during every game, we would figure out what was going on and clean it up. Even though they were kicking our butts, there was never any time when we felt we weren't going to break away."

The defense forced another punt and the Redskins began another touchdown march. This time, running back Danny Lewis scored from the 2 early in the fourth quarter to cut the lead to 24-20.

Dallas lost more than just its 11-point lead on this drive. Lilly, who would earn his third straight

Pro Bowl berth at season's end, sprained his left knee. He was lost for the rest of the game. So, too, was the Cowboys' pass rush.

"When Lilly is in there," Cowboys secondary coach Dick Nolan said, "they've got to double- and triple-team him, pick him up as he rolls through one guy after another. He just busts up the pass pocket."

Dallas' troubles lessened on Washington's next possession when linebacker Dave Edwards intercepted Jurgensen. Three plays later, Meredith threw a 53-yard touchdown pass to receiver Frank Clarke. With just under six minutes remaining, the Cowboys led, 31-20.

Jurgensen struck quickly. Passes of 15 to Mitchell, 39 to receiver Angelo Coia and 10 to Mitchell produced a touchdown with 3:32 left.

Once more the defense stiffened, despite Dallas' 56-yard kickoff return to the Washington 41. Villanueva would miss a 45-yard field goal attempt and, with 1:41 remaining, the Redskins were 80 yards from victory.

They chewed that up in a hurry. Even when something bad happened, so, too did something good. Jurgensen fumbled on first down, but recovered to gain nine yards.

Rookie tight end Jerry Smith induced a 19-yard pass interference penalty and followed that with a 22-yard reception to the Dallas 40.

Frustration mounted on the Dallas sideline as Landry and Nolan argued about coverages. Landry ordered Nolan to change defenses. But Landry's man-to-man coverage failed as Mitchell beat Green for a 35-yard reception at the 5 — snagging a low pass while nearly bent over — with 1:14 to play. Landry, who reportedly did not talk to Nolan after the game, called that "the play of the game."

Still facing a man coverage, Jurgensen hit Coia for the go-ahead touchdown.

"We were trying everything," Landry said. "Blitzes, three-man rushes, the works. We were desperate. But Jurgensen was as hot as he's ever been ... and I've always thought he was the best passer in the conference."

But the Cowboys, still with 1:04 remaining, had explosive talent as well. And they nearly answered with a last-minute score of their own. Six plays, including two sacks, produced eight yards. Meredith then connected with Hayes for a 35-yard gain to the Washington 34. Seven seconds remained.

Villanueva lined up for the game-tying attempt.

There, another Redskins trio saved the day. Huff and 14-year veteran lineman Fred Williams cleared an opening for 6-foot-3 defensive back Lonnie Sanders, who jumped over them and blocked the kick.

"They pulled their men and gave me a chance to run through," Sanders said. "Anybody could have blocked that kick."

Dallas recovered to win three straight to finish 7-7 and, starting in 1966, began a string of eight straight playoff appearances. The Redskins finished 6-8 and fired coach Bill McPeak. The playoffs remained a dream.

But at least McPeak had guided the best comeback in club history, thanks to Jurgensen. In the end, the crowd cheered the quarterback, and the offense, loudly. Mitchell caught six passes for 99 yards and Taylor grabbed seven for 139. Meanwhile, Jurgensen completed 17-of-22 passes for 303 yards and two touchdowns in the second half. He finished 26-of-42 for 411 yards and three scores.

"It was," McPeak said, "one of the greatest quarterbacking exhibitions ever."

REDSKINS 34, COWBOYS 31

	1	2	3	4	TOTAL
COWBOYS	14	7	3	7	31
REDSKINS	0	6	7	21	34

◆ **FIRST QUARTER**
D - Dunn 6 pass from Meredith (Villanueva kick), D 7-0
D - Green 5 run with fumble (Villanueva kick), D 14-0

◆ **SECOND QUARTER**
D - Gaechter 60 return of blocked FG attempt (Villanueva kick), D 21-0
W - Taylor 26 pass from Jurgensen (kick blocked), D 21-6

◆ **THIRD QUARTER**
D - Villanueva 30 FG, D 24-6
W - Jurgensen 1 run (Jencks kick), D 24-13

◆ **FOURTH QUARTER**
W - Lewis 2 run (Jencks kick), D 24-20
D - Clarke 53 pass from Meredith (Villanueva kick), D 31-20
W - Mitchell 10 pass from Jurgensen (Jencks kick), D 31-27
W - Coia 5 pass from Jurgensen (Jencks kick), W 34-31

Dallas quarterback Don Meredith and coach Tom Landry helped vault the Cowboys into the NFL's elite by the end of the 1960s.

Nov. 13, 1966

A Real Dandy

Cowboys 31, Redskins 3

The Dallas Cowboys were not yet *the Dallas Cowboys*, nowhere even near "Next Year's Champions," the anvil-heavy nickname they were to be burdened with for forthcoming championship failures until legitimizing their NFL existence by winning Super Bowl VI.

This was only 1966, and Dallas was but a 6-year-old franchise mired in mediocrity, and playing in this allegedly rough-and-tumble Old West city stained nationwide for allowing President John F. Kennedy to be assassinated in its downtown midst. The Grassy Knoll certainly was better known than Cowboys coach Tom Landry, the former New York Giants assistant given the club's reins at its 1960 inception. Entering their seventh season, the Cowboys had yet to produce a winning record, going a franchise-best 7-7 in 1965, which qualified them anyway for the Playoff Bowl, no more than an NFL consolation game to appease second-place finishers. Dallas even lost that game to Baltimore, 35-0.

Don Meredith was just some quarterback from SMU. Dan Reeves, a kid out of South Carolina. Cornerback Mel Renfro just another defensive back. Pete Gent? Walt Garrison? Chuck Howley? The best known Cowboy just might have been wide receiver Bob Hayes, more so for his 1964 Olympic gold medals in the 100 meters and 400-meter relay, than for his football accomplishments. Hayes was known as "The World's Fastest Human" for lowering the 100-meter world record to 10-flat.

"You have to remember," Landry said, "we didn't have anything going for us until 1966."

So the Cowboys strolled into D.C. Stadium with a 5-2-1 record, in second place behind the St. Louis Cardinals (7-1-1) and on the cusp of their first winning season with six games remaining. They had begun the season with four consecutive victories, and added to the three straight to finish 1965, had established a franchise-high, seven-game, regular-season winning streak.

But on this sunny day with the temperature near 50 degrees in the nation's capital, here were the Redskins, clinging to hopes that NFL great Otto Graham, in his first year as their coach, could revitalize this downtrodden organization. And while they stood just 5-4, the Redskins had beaten the Cowboys in two of the past three meetings, including a miraculous comeback when quarterback Sonny Jurgensen erased 21-0 and 31-20 Dallas leads – the last with five minutes remaining – to put a 34-31 bruise on the Cowboys budding egos in 1965.

Dallas still was a franchise finding its way.

And as late afternoon set in on D.C. Stadium, it appeared the search would continue, the old master Jurgensen once again passing the Cowboys dizzy and into apparent submission. Similar to the last time the two teams had met, the Cowboys grabbed an early lead, this time 21-6, mostly thanks to the blossoming Meredith-to-Hayes combination. The two were spectacular.

"The best day I ever had," Bob Hayes said.

This would be the best day any Cowboys receiver ever had, Hayes setting the single-game franchise record with 246 yards, needing only nine catches to do so. Two of those catches were electrifying.

Hayes first created separation in a 7-6 game by teaming with Meredith on a 52-yard touchdown pass late in the second quarter.

"We caught them in a blitz, and we knew they would be blitzing because we studied so much in the classroom, coach Landry intellectualizing every damn play," Hayes said. "We had to know what he knew. We knew it was a blitz when [cornerback] Lonnie Sanders came up a little closer and played me on the inside. When it was not a blitz, he played me on the outside. And [running back] Don Perkins was the one who made the play go. Don picked up all those bad guys blitzing, and gave me the chance to run under the ball."

You think the Redskins would have learned. After all, Hayes produced 12 receiving touchdowns his rookie year during the 14-game season, and was well on his way in 1966 toward establishing the club's single-season record for most yards receiving (1,232), a record which stood for 25 years until Michael Irvin went for 1,523 (16 games) in 1991. Not only that, Hayes would stretch his single-season touchdown receptions record from 12 to 13, which remains a

Cowboys record. More than that, Hayes would change the landscape of NFL defenses, his speed forcing teams from predominately man-to-man coverages into bracketing zones.

Unfortunately for Sanders, this change did not come soon enough. The Cowboys first possession of the second half, leading 14-6, began at their own 5.

"Dandy Don got in the huddle and said, 'Man, I want to go over there and drink some water,'" Hayes remembered. "Dandy Don was one of those quarterbacks when he was ready to go, he'd be ready to go. He just said, 'Come on Bobby, you got to do it. Now you got to catch this pass.'"

Everyone stayed in to block, and Meredith just aired it out, gambling that the "World's Fastest Human" could outrun this mere human assigned to cover him.

"I still watch the play quite a bit now," Hayes said. "He threw the ball to me, and I just ran under the ball, caught it and straightened out. Lonnie thought I was going to the outside. But I ran right in front of him on a fly pattern."

In 1964, nations of sprinters couldn't catch Hayes from behind. Certainly Sanders would not as the Cowboys took a 21-6 lead.

But again, it would seem, the Cowboys had only given Jurgensen something to shoot at, the "Redhead" throwing for three second-half touchdowns, and finishing with 347 yards passing. Not to be outdone, Jurgensen connected with Taylor on his own 78-yard scoring strike.

"I was going across the middle, and they had me all wrapped up," Taylor said. "I thought I was dead. But the safeties, the cornerback and linebacker all collided at the same time. The next thing I knew, they're all laying on the ground and I'm still standing there."

Taylor would catch another touchdown pass, an 18-yarder to give the Redskins an improbable 30-28 lead with 5:38 remaining. He would break the Redskins' single-game receiving yards record with 199, and his second touchdown forged a fourth lead change.

Yet there would be an astonishing fifth lead change.

Only 1:30 was left to play. The ball rested ominously on the Dallas 3. The Cowboys still trailed 30-28. They had no timeouts, and barely more hope. After all, Meredith had played the entire second half with a right thumb swollen and purple. He was throwing basically with four fingers. Kicker Danny Villanueva's longest field goal that season had been 42 yards. The Cowboys needed to reach at least the 35 to have a chance. That was 62 yards away. The goal post was 97 yards away.

Future greatness seemed an eternity away.

"I'm thinking: The game is over," Cowboys cornerback Mel Renfro said. "I mean the game is over. We had lost. No question about that. No time. No timeouts."

Meredith knew the seconds were precious, so he began drawing up plays in the sideline dirt before the offensive unit took the field. He ordered all plays to be run from the club's "orange formation," and to simplify matters, he junked all that fancy pre-snap movement, snapping the ball with the same count. Great, but even left tackle Tony Liscio was seen blessing himself with the sign of the cross as he entered the huddle. He understood higher intervention was required.

"Don just said, 'We're going to win this damn game,'" Hayes recalled.

Meredith might have come of age during these 90 seconds. The Cowboys definitely did. On first down, with the Redskins in a prevent defense, Meredith connected with Gent for 26 yards, but Gent

In the 1960s, the Cowboys had 20 players combine for 54 Pro Bowl appearances while the Redskins had 22 players total 40 trips. Defensive tackle Bob Lilly led Dallas with seven Pro Bowls, followed by cornerback Mel Renfro with six and linebacker Chuck Howley and defensive end George Andrie with five each. For Washington, quarterback Sonny Jurgensen, linebacker Chris Hanburger and receiver Charley Taylor each made four appearances.

failed to get out of bounds. The clock was running. From the 29, Meredith ran for 12 yards and a first down, swerving out of bounds with assistance from Redskins linebacker Sam Huff.

"Their defensive line had been putting a lot of pressure on us, so Meredith had told Gent, 'I'm going to roll to the right, and you just run to the right, like a sideline route,' and Meredith just rolled to the right and kept throwing to Pete," Hayes said.

Just 59 seconds remained, and Meredith's pass from the 41 to Garrison fell incomplete. That took four seconds. He went to Garrison again on second down, this time for only one yard, but Garrison got out of bounds at the 42, nine yards short of a first down. Only 48 seconds were left.

"My one yard probably won the game, right?" Garrison sarcastically said. "[Don] Perkins, God love him, didn't have the greatest hands in the world, so I got to play on a lot of third-and-longs and passing situations."

This was third-and-long, but incredibly, Meredith connected with Gent for 25 yards to the Washington 33, defensive back Rickie Harris dragging him down. With the clock ticking toward 33 seconds, at least the Cowboys had given Villanueva a chance if they moved no closer.

But Meredith, the swashbuckler that he was, ran again for the sideline, mainly intending to stop the clock. He gained six yards for his trouble, but after stepping out of bounds with 19 seconds remaining Redskins linebacker John Reger, frustrated by Meredith's elusiveness and daring, blasted him five yards beyond the sideline. Flag. Fifteen-yard personal foul penalty. Advance the ball to the Washington 12.

"I figured we had a chance now," Renfro said

Landry would take no chances from the 12, with so little time left and no timeouts. He ordered a Villanueva 20-yard field-goal attempt, "and to this day I remember Taco [Villanueva] kicking that winning field goal," Garrison said of the climax to the Cowboys' 31-30 victory.

"When we won that game at Washington, that was the highlight of my career, and I could only compare that victory with the victory in the Olympics," Hayes said, referring to the 400-meter relay triumph in Tokyo. "I remember in Tokyo we were five to seven yards behind, and the French team had

been telling everyone on our team all week, 'You guys only have Hayes.' "

Turns out, that is all the USA team needed. The French and the British were in no better shape than Sanders. Hayes blistered the final leg in a flesh-chilling 8.6 seconds, leading the USA team to a gold medal and world record (39-flat).

"After we won," Hayes said, "Paul Drayton of Villanova went up to the French team and said, 'The only person we needed was Hayes.' "

On this day, the Cowboys needed Hayes and Meredith and Gent and Garrison and then some. And little did they know, maybe even a guardian angel.

Back in Dallas as the Cowboys whooped it up in D. C. Stadium, Robert Summerall was heading out of his apartment to celebrate the Cowboys' victory he had just watched on TV. But Summerall noticed something unusual – a tiny tot in the apartment complex swimming pool flailing for his life. Summerall rushed into the pool fully clothed to save the youngster who had fallen in and gone under.

The little boy was 2-year-old Timmy Villanueva, Danny's son.

"If we had lost the game maybe [Summerall] wouldn't have gone out," said then–Cowboys public relations director Al Ward. "Makes you wonder, doesn't it?"

And if the Cowboys had lost the game, maybe they never would have become *the Cowboys*. Makes you wonder, doesn't it?

COWBOYS 31, REDSKINS 30

	1	2	3	4	TOTAL
COWBOYS	7	7	7	10	31
REDSKINS	6	0	17	7	30

◆ **FIRST QUARTER**
W - Gogolak 35 FG, W 3-0
D - Meredith 1 run (Villanueva kick), D 7-3
W - Gogolak 33 FG, D 7-6

◆ **SECOND QUARTER**
D - Hayes 52 pass from Meredith (Villanueva kick), D 14-6

◆ **THIRD QUARTER**
D - Hayes 95 pass from Meredith (Villanueva kick), D 21-6
W - Smith 4 pass from Jurgensen (Gogolak kick), D 21-13
W - Taylor 78 pass Jurgensen (Gogolak kick), D 21-20
W - Gogolak 11 FG, W 23-21

◆ **FOURTH QUARTER**
D - Reeves 1 run (Villanueva kick), D 28-23
W - Taylor 18 pass from Jurgensen (Gogolak kick), W 30-28
D - Villanueva 20 FG, D 31-30

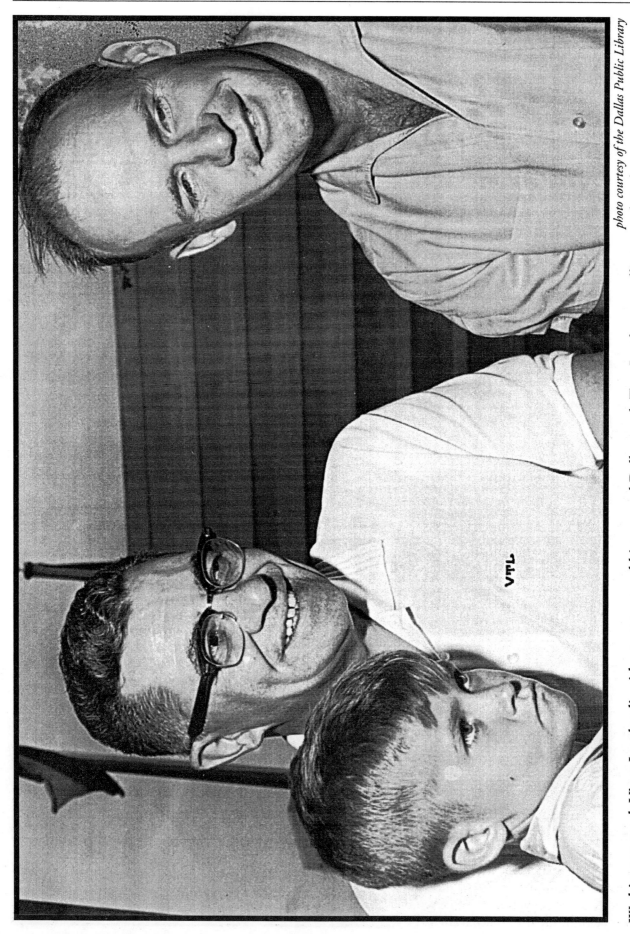

photo courtesy of the Dallas Public Library

Washington coach Vince Lombardi, with an arm around his son, and Dallas coach Tom Landry were allies turned rivals.

Nov. 16, 1969

A Hill Of A Day

Cowboys 41, Redskins 28

The man with the gap-toothed grin had changed sidelines, gone from Title Town USA to Capital Town USA; from Green Bay to Washington D.C., where titles were reserved for government heads, not Redskins.

The Washington Redskins had not enjoyed a winning season since 1955, and it did not matter who the coach was, Joe Kuharich, Mike Nixon, Bill McPeak or Otto Graham. They had not won a division title since 1945, and no world championship since the war-torn 1942 season. Even Graham, the legendary Cleveland quarterback appointed head coach and general manager in 1966, couldn't turn the corner in his three seasons, at best going 7-7 that first year and at worst going 5-9 in 1968, his final year.

Drastic times call for miracles, and before the death of Redskins founder George Preston Marshall Aug. 9, 1969, club president Edward Bennett Williams coaxed the gap-toothed man, Vince Lombardi, out of his cushy, yet uncomfortable one-year front-office stay in Green Bay, to coach again. To coach the Washington Redskins.

The Redskins might not have won a division title in 23 seasons, but now at least they had a coach who had won world titles, Lombardi claiming five NFL championships during his nine years in Green Bay. The hard-nosed Lombardi won the last three of those championships consecutively (1965-67), finishing off the latter two seasons by beating the AFL champs in the first two Super Bowls before heading upstairs in 1968. It would take the Packers 29 years to win another Super Bowl.

Don't you know groans echoed across the state of Texas on Feb. 7, 1969, when the Redskins hired Vincent T. Lombardi to be their coach and executive vice-president. Don't you know people south of the Red River cried, now the Redskins have the guy the Cowboys just can't beat.

Too fresh in the minds of the Cowboys and their growing legion of followers were the back-to-back NFL Championship Game losses to Lombardi's Packers. Dallas lost a Cotton Bowl

shootout, 34-27, in 1966, the game ending with a Don Meredith pass on fourth-and-goal at the 2 being intercepted in the end zone by safety Tom Brown. As if that wasn't painful enough, the Cowboys nearly froze to death the following year in what became known as the Ice Bowl, Packers quarterback Bart Starr sneaking in for the climactic touchdown from the 1 in the final seconds with no timeouts remaining for the 21-17 victory.

Thirty years later, that loss lingers in Dallas.

"A great game for us, having played the legends, and having beaten them until the last damn play," said former Cowboys president Tex Schramm, still with noticeable disdain. "It still pisses me off. Lombardi took a gamble … and the guard [Jerry Kramer] went early."

Now Lombardi was in Dallas' face again. As a coach, he had never lost a game to the Cowboys. Lombardi was 6-0. Cowboys coach Tom Landry had never beaten a Lombardi-coached team. He was 0-6.

"And when we lost those games in '66 and '67, we ended up as the team that couldn't win the big one," Landry said.

So as regular season games go, this Nov. 16 clash was a relatively big one, the Cowboys 7-1, the Redskins 4-2-2, and on the verge of capturing that elusive winning season with six games remaining. Even the President of the United States was lending the Redskins advice, Richard M. Nixon saying at a Veterans Day function which Cowboys owner Clint Murchison just happened to be attending, "They need some defense … could beat Dallas."

The presidential aid moved the normally stoic, but staunch Republican Landry to respond, sending off a telegram, streaking some color on this budding rivalry: "I agree with you on everything but your football prognostication."

Nixon had a point. The Redskins were in dire need of defense, even with Lombardi around. Here they were ranked last in rushing defense, and here the Cowboys were, coming to RFK Stadium with rookie sensation Calvin Hill leading the league with

657 rushing yards and averaging 5.1 yards a carry.

"Even the Little Sisters of the Poor could run on us," Lombardi had said at the time.

Little Sisters, Redskins … the Cowboys didn't care. They just wanted to run, and beat the Redskins … finally beat Lombardi.

So they turned to one so young, the 22-year-old Hill, their first-round draft choice out of Yale, and then big play after big play to finally knock that crooked smile off Lombardi's face. Hill rushed 27 times for 150 yards, both numbers setting Dallas single-game records. And to think Lombardi told his Redskins before kickoff, "Intimidate this team to win." Hill also would return three kick-offs for 100 yards and catch two passes for 35 more.

That's 285 total yards from the kid so nervous the night before he barely slept.

"I had grown up in Baltimore, so we were huge Colts fans and rabid, anti-anything Washington," said Hill, who would go on to play for the Redskins (1976-77) after a brief stint in the World Football League. "So I wanted to beat them in the worst way. The game was only 32 miles from my home, and I had lots of folks at the game, so I was excited."

Lombardi or not, this had become one of those typical Cowboys-Redskins game at RFK Stadium: The Cowboys streaked to a 24-7 lead early in the second quarter before Sonny Jurgensen would have his say – and way – with the Cowboys' defense. It was Hill's first of two touchdowns, a 3-yard run, establishing this Cowboys lead, the biggest they would enjoy this game.

"Two things stand out about that game," Hill said. "One, I remember getting knocked out of bounds on the Redskins' side, and I mean really knocked out, and there I am on my stomach and I'm looking at a pair of shoes. And when I look up, I see it's Lombardi, and he has that ol' quizzical smile on his face, and I remember thinking, 'That's Vince Lombardi,' and for a moment there, I lost my perspective on where I was.

"Also, I remember shifting, you know how we used a multiple offense. And this time we used a double shift, and we shifted from an I to a brown formation. We had this brown formation that was up and over. Fullback Walt [Garrison] shifted over to where the halfback would normally be on the weak side and I shifted up into a slot. And I remember Redskins linebacker Sam Huff started screaming to Vince on the sideline, 'Vince, Vince what do I call?' And he eventually called a timeout.

"I remember being mystified, here was the great Sam Huff, and he was confused. So that sort of made me feel less sensitive about being confused about what was going on."

What went on in this game was big play after big play:

• Cowboys quarterback Craig Morton, playing with a painful shoulder, hit Lance Rentzel for a 65-yard touchdown.

• Cowboys defensive end Larry Cole intercepted a Mike Gaechter-tipped Jurgensen pass, and returned it 41 yards for a touchdown, the third consecutive game Cole had scored a touchdown against the Redskins. "I had a big slow guard trying to catch me, and I got in in the nick of time," Cole said.

• Bob Hayes returned a punt 50 yards to the Washington 3, setting up Hill's first touchdown.

• Jurgensen teaming up with receiver Charley Taylor for an 88-yard touchdown pass, cutting the

Vince Lombardi (offensive coordinator) and Tom Landry (defensive coordinator) worked together as New York Giants assistant coaches under Jim Lee Howell from 1954-58. The Giants won the championship in 1956, beating the Chicago Bears, 47-7. Two years later, the Baltimore Colts defeated New York, 23-17, in overtime in perhaps the most important NFL title game. New York never had a losing season with these two assistants.

Lombardi left in 1959 to become Green Bay's coach. Landry took a similar position with the expansion Cowboys in 1960.

lead to 10 midway through the second quarter.

• Washington's Rickie Harris returned a punt 83 yards for the touchdown that would have given the Redskins a 28-27 early, third-quarter lead, only to have a clipping penalty on Chris Hanburger nullify the score. "I didn't think it was a very good call because I felt I had my head was in front of [Dave Edwards], and yeah, the guy did turn, but the refs missed that," Hanburger said.

• Cowboys cornerback Cornell Green blocked a 48-yard Curt Knight field goal attempt.

• Renfro, at his own 8, intercepted a Jurgensen bomb intended for receiver Bob Long with Dallas leading 34-28 early in the fourth quarter.

• Chuck Howley intercepted a Jurgensen pass intended for Long at the Cowboys 11 on the very next possession, later claiming, "I couldn't believe it. Jurgensen must not have seen me."

• Renfro, almost fittingly, ended the game by intercepting Jurgensen's final, desperation pass as the clock expired.

The Cowboys had finally beaten Lombardi.

And Landry, after getting off to that horrendous 0-11-1 first-year start and 18-46-4 record over his first five seasons, finally had evened his and the franchise's record at 64-64 in this, their 10th season.

"Not just [beating] Lombardi, but I remember any time we beat Washington was a big deal," said Garrison, who had his hands full blocking for Hill that day. "That's what makes rivalries."

As for Lombardi, he felt moved to apologize, saying afterward, "I'm sorry we couldn't win for the President. But they just had too many guns for us."

As for Jurgensen, who passed for 338 yards, with four touchdowns and four interceptions, he would suffer a mild concussion after the game when he swerved to miss another vehicle, rolling the Mercedes he was driving.

As for the Redskins, they would go on to break their drought that year, finishing 7-5-2 for their first winning season in 15 years.

As for Hill, he would not join Chicago's Beattie Feathers (1934) as the only NFL rookies to rush for more than 1,000 yards. With five games to go, Hill needed only 193 yards to reach 1,000, and just 138 to break Don Perkins' club single-sea-son rushing record. He had averaged nearly 90 yards a game after nine games.

But Hill didn't get there, having broken a sesamoid bone in his right foot, unbeknownst to him.

"We thought I had a turf toe," Hill said. "Midway in the third or early in the fourth quarter I shifted, and when I landed I felt a strange sensation in my foot. I thought it was a sprain. I wasn't quite sure what it was."

Hill attempted to play the next two games, but couldn't perform very well. Dan Reeves started instead in Game 11.

"We tried a different shoe, and I still couldn't play," Hill said. "I mean I was trying anything, you know, horse liniment, people were sending me stuff to rub on the toe. So I went to see a podiatrist in town, and he examined it, and said, 'Well, no wonder it hurts. You have a fracture.' "

Hill would gain just 135 yards after that Washington game, four short of establishing the club's single-season rushing record, 48 short of joining Feathers and not near enough to hold off Chicago's Gale Sayers for the NFL rushing title.

And as for the Cowboys, yes, they beat Lombardi, and did so only one more time, winning the 1969 rematch, 20-10, in the final game. That would be the final game of Lombardi's life. He died of cancer Sept. 3, 1970, leaving a gap not only in Washington, but throughout the National Football League.

COWBOYS 41, REDSKINS 28					
	1	2	3	4	TOTAL
COWBOYS	17	10	7	7	41
REDSKINS	7	14	7	0	28

◆ **FIRST QUARTER**
D - Clark 36 FG, D 3-0
W - Smith 27 pass from Jurgensen (Knight kick), W 7-3
D - Rentzel 65 pass from Morton (Clark kick), D 10-7
D - Cole 41 interception return (Clark kick), D 17-7

◆ **SECOND QUARTER**
D - Hill 3 run (Clark kick), D 24-7
W - Taylor 88 pass from Jurgensen (Knight kick), D 24-14
D - Clark 14 FG, D 27-14
W - Smith 11 pass from Jurgensen (Knight kick), D 27-21

◆ **THIRD QUARTER**
D - Hill 7 run (Clark kick), D 34-21
W - Smith 20 pass from Jurgensen (Knight kick), D 34-28

◆ **FOURTH QUARTER**
D - Reeves 4 run (Clark kick), D 41-28

Sonny Jurgensen

The Cotton Bowl was packed with Dallas Cowboys fans ready for a brawl. The rivalry with the Washington Redskins was already intense by the mid-1960s, and both players and fans were pumped for the game.

But Washington quarterback Sonny Jurgensen and Dallas quarterback Don Meredith seemed oblivious to the howling crowd while waiting at midfield for the coin toss. Instead of trading pregame barbs, they discussed Meredith's alligator boots which Jurgensen had admired earlier that day.

"Meredith asked me what size shoes did I wear," Jurgensen said. "After I told him, he said he'd send me a pair of alligator boots. He did, too."

Jurgensen loved beating the Cowboys. Mostly, it was the challenge of defeating a team that made the playoffs six of first seven years that the "Redhead" started against them while the Redskins managed only one winning season. He passed for more than 300 yards five times against Dallas, in-

photo courtesy of the Washington Redskins

cluding twice in 1966. Jurgensen was only 4-10 against the Cowboys, and the Redskins needed to score between 27 to 34 points in each of their four victories.

"We had to outscore them to beat them," Jurgensen said of the many shootouts and close games. "When you could beat a Tom Landry-coached team, it was a good feeling. That defensive line was rough. Their secondary was tough. We had real battles."

Dallas receiver Bob Hayes admitted the Cowboys sometimes felt helpless against Jurgensen.

"When Sonny got hot, he could really thread the needle," Hayes said. "There were probably a half dozen games during our rivalry with Sonny and Charley Taylor where they lit up the athletic arena with their passing game. Along with Sonny Jurgensen, I think Joe Namath and Johnny Unitas were the greatest pure passers I've ever played against. Sonny could throw the ball by you. He wasn't bashful at all. There were many occasions when they struck like lightning. I mean we would hold them for two or three quarters, and then in one quarter they would score three times and blow us out of the water. You could never relax against Sonny."

Jurgensen was practically unstoppable when the teams met twice in 28 days near the end of the 1966 season. Jurgensen completed 26-of-43 passes for 347 yards with three touchdowns in a 31-30 loss. In the rematch at the Cotton Bowl, the Redskins won, 34-31, behind Jurgensen's 18-of-33 passing for 308 yards with three touchdowns and one interception. And in the second 1965 meeting, Jurgensen completed 26-of-43 for 411 yards with three touchdowns and two interceptions in a 34-31 Redskins victory.

But Jurgensen's favorite memory against Dallas comes from a photo still hanging in his Alexandria, Va. home. Cowboys defensive tackle Bob Lilly is shown literally knocked upside down by Redskins center Len Hauss.

"Lilly's feet are straight up in the air where Hauss undercut him," Jurgensen said. "Lilly never said a word, and on the next play came right back at me. Lilly just came and came and came."

So did Jurgensen.

Don Meredith

It was pure perfection. A play that worked exactly as Dallas quarterback Don Meredith envisioned.

"We couldn't get a thing going all day," Meredith told Parkway magazine. "Finally, in the huddle I said, 'Everybody block and Bobby Hayes go deep.' At the snap, I knew it was right. They all rushed, and I go back, look one way, then another. Sure enough, Hayes had split 'em. Wow!"

It was a 95-yard touchdown, the longest pass in Cowboys history and the difference in beating the Washington Redskins 31-30 on Nov. 13, 1966.

"You know it's a real thing when that play goes off in your head and you know just how hard, just how precise to throw the ball," Meredith said. "And you let it go like I did and he didn't break stride. Whoosh, watch him run. That was a nice thrill."

But it was more than just a touchdown, more than just a victory. The electrifying triumph over the Redskins helped the Cowboys finish 10-3-1 en route to losing the 1966 NFL Championship to the Green Bay Packers. After six years of struggling, both Meredith and the Cowboys were finally winners.

No Cowboy shouldered more pressure during the early years than Meredith. The Cotton Bowl was his home for 13 seasons. In fact, he had already played four years there for Southern Methodist as a two-time all-American passer before signing a personal services contract with Cowboys owner Clint Murchison as the team's first player. Indeed, some say Meredith became a local sports legend in first grade by scoring 53 points in a basketball tournament.

When the horror of the 1963 assassination of President John F. Kennedy befell Dallas, locals looked to football for their escape. They looked to Meredith. Now living in Santa Fe, N.M. and declining interviews, Meredith admitted in a 1983 profile that the pressure of helping the city overcome Kennedy's murder proved nearly overwhelming. Indeed, the Cowboys had to play the Cleveland Browns after learning in the locker room of the murder of Kennedy assassin Lee Harvey Oswald.

"I was going through some severe growing pains," he said. "So was the city. So was the nation. Everybody was really, really frustrated. Dallas began to change almost overnight. It seemed like the cork finally blew and all the craziness came gushing out. Everything was weird. Vietnam, [President] Lyndon B. Johnson being a Texan and all those rumors linking him to the assassination. For the first time in my life, I began to question structures, parental guidance, authority, how to live. And there I found myself in a public position . . . Dallas Cowboys quarterback."

The Cowboys twice led the NFL in offense during Meredith's nine seasons before his 1969 retirement. Despite injuries and a lackluster team for the first half of his career, Meredith earned respect for his often gritty perfor-

photo courtesy of the Dallas Cowboys

mances. He was inducted into the Cowboys' Ring of Honor in 1976.

"Don was very competitive," said Redskins quarterback Sonny Jurgensen. "Don was very disciplined . . . he just liked to play."

Said Cowboys coach Tom Landry: "Don and Walt Garrison were the two toughest players I ever had. Guys who could take punishment and perform."

Both Landry and Meredith admitted their relationship was strained, but it didn't prevent a mutual respect.

"Don and I were never real close," Landry said. "Not that I don't like Don — I like him fine — but you'd have to say we really are on different wavelengths."

Redskins receiver Roy Jefferson blows past Cowboys safety Charlie Waters en route to a 50-yard touchdown. Waters and his teammates had trouble catching Washington all game.

Oct. 3, 1971

Stinging In The Rain

Redskins 20, Cowboys 16

The Dallas Cowboys entered the NFL as an expansion team in 1960, but it didn't take them long to join the rest of the league in looking down on the lowly Washington Redskins. Dallas was just 5-8-1 in 1962: 1-0-1 against Washington and 4-8 against everyone else.

"They felt they were better than us as an expansion team and I guess there was some truth to that," said Hall of Fame receiver Bobby Mitchell, a Redskin from 1962-68.

By 1971, Dallas' five straight winning seasons equalled Washington's total since the end of World War II. And the Cowboys had won the last six meetings with the Redskins by an average of 16 points.

However, Washington was now being led by a man on a mission. George Allen had taken over the Redskins as coach and general manager after being fired by the Los Angeles Rams despite five straight non-losing seasons.

Allen, the defensive mastermind behind the Chicago Bears' 1963 NFL title, was coming East to win the Super Bowl.

"The Redskins knew the road to the NFC East championship went through the Cowboys," said Dallas safety Charlie Waters, whose team would go on to crush Miami, 24-3, in Super Bowl VI.

"George said they were the elite team and if we were going to win the division, we would have to beat them," said Washington quarterback Billy Kilmer, the first player Allen traded for after assuming command. "Dallas had a lot more talent than we did. We would have to beat them on emotion and hard play."

Allen, who would become even more focused and frenzied than usual during Dallas Week, took care of the emotion.

"George could motivate a team," said fullback Charley Harraway. "He was so emotional, he would get the whole team going. We had a bunch of veterans and we would look at each other when George was giving us one of his rah-rah talks and we would be smiling and jumping around the room like little kids. It was corny, but it was fun."

And Allen's trades would help ensure the hard play. When the coach arrived, Washington's offense was already strong with quarterback Sonny Jurgensen, receiver Charley Taylor, halfback Larry Brown and tight end Jerry Smith, all veterans of at least two Pro Bowls. But the defense had just two top players, linebacker Chris Hanburger and cornerback Pat Fischer.

So Allen rebuilt the defense. He traded for ends Ron McDole of Buffalo and Verlon Biggs of the New York Jets as well as plenty of his former Rams: tackle Diron Talbert, linebackers Jack Pardee, Maxie Baughn and Myron Pottios and safety Richie Petitbon. The offense would be supplemented by Kilmer from New Orleans, receivers Clifton McNeil from the New York Giants and Roy Jefferson from Baltimore as well as yet another ex-Ram, guard John Wilbur.

"Dallas had more talent," Harraway said. "They were automated. They were light/years ahead of other teams in terms of the way they did things. But we had several superstars who could rise to the occasion. And we had more character. And character plays a big part in success."

While the Cowboys concentrated on building through the draft – only four of their 1971 starters weren't homegrown – the Redskins were a mishmash. Many had been unwanted by their former teams. How quickly could a team with nine new starters and a revamped coaching staff come together?

"I wasn't worried about how long it would take guys from all over to jell," Jefferson said. "We were veterans. I knew as long as guys were attentive to detail and they were professional, we could win immediately."

But when Jurgensen broke his shoulder in preseason, the prospects for immediate success seemed doomed. After all, Kilmer hadn't been the same since being badly injured in a 1963 car accident.

"No one, including Billy, had any idea that Sonny wasn't going to be the key to our offense," said defensive tackle Bill Brundige. "And when he goes down, you look around and say, 'Oh my God, it's going to be Billy. What the hell can he do?'"

The question was still being asked after the defense forced seven turnovers in the opening 24-17 victory over St. Louis and even after Kilmer completed 23-of-32 passes for 309 yards in the 30-3 rout of the Giants the next week. Washington may have been 2-0 for the first time since 1955, but Dallas was up next.

The Cowboys were also 2-0, having beaten Buffalo, 49-37, and Philadelphia, 42-7. And with no 1970 playoff team on its schedule, Dallas was already thinking Super Bowl again. Certainly, Washington wouldn't be much of an obstacle.

"They had these worn-out players and their talent level wasn't nearly what ours was," said Dallas defensive end Larry Cole. "With Billy Kilmer at quarterback, you said, 'How could we possibly lose the game?'"

But Allen and Kilmer had a formula.

"We had just come off two good wins and we were all fired up," Kilmer said. "We were determined not to lose. I knew there was a lot of pressure on me. George just said, 'Look Billy. Just do your job. Don't try to win the game yourself. Use the talent you've got [around you].'"

And on your defense.

"The Cowboys had some great players, but we just outsmarted them," McDole said. "We had Pat Fischer and Richie Petitbon, guys who were coaches on the field. Today, they run guys in and out, but most of us played every down on defense. We had the experience to make up for having lost half a step."

As the game began in the rain of the Cotton Bowl, Kilmer handed off on the first three plays. Harraway went off right tackle for three yards. Brown took a pitch around right end for 13. And then Kilmer surprisingly called Harraway's number again.

"Usually I didn't get the ball twice in the whole first quarter," said Harraway, normally the lead blocker for Brown, the NFL rushing leader in 1970.

But Harraway got it this time on a weakside sweep from the Dallas 43. Harraway had reached about midfield when Taylor gave him all the room he needed with a devastating block on Waters.

"Here comes Taylor across the field, looking like a stroll in the park and he hits Waters with a forearm to the face and knocks him off his feet," Brundige said. "They had to carry him off the field."

But not until Harraway had raced 57 yards to give the 10-point underdogs a quick 7-0 lead.

"I don't think I was even touched, the blocking was so good," Harraway said.

"I didn't go out there trying to hurt people, but I wanted to knock them on their butts," Taylor said.

"That set the tone for the entire game," Kilmer said.

Dallas running back Calvin Hill, who would later play for Allen's Redskins, said the Cowboys didn't play well that day, but they did learn a lesson.

"You couldn't be too cute with a George Allen team," Hill said. "If you tried to outsmart them, because they had old guys who had seen a lot and understood the game, you would get in trouble. But if you really slugged it out with them at first, then you would get an advantage."

The Cowboys' early slugging proved fruitless. They kept the ball for the next 15 plays but failed to score when a Redskin got a hand on Mike Clark's 48-yard field goal try. Clark's 22-yarder narrowed the gap to 7-3 early in the second quarter, but the score wouldn't stay close for long.

After an exchange of punts, Washington took over at midfield. Kilmer, who had thrown just one pass because of the rain, decided to take a shot

---

In the decade before George Allen's arrival as coach, the Redskins compiled a record of 51-81-8 with one winning season. Under Allen, Washington went 67-30-1 with seven winning seasons and five postseason appearances, including one trip to the Super Bowl.

Allen passed on his quest for success to his children. Son Bruce is the senior administrator with the Oakland Raiders and another son, George, is the governor of Virginia.

against cornerback Herb Adderly, a former Green Bay star now nearing the end of his career.

"Their corners felt they could cover us one-on-one," Jefferson said. "But I had whipped Herb when I was with Pittsburgh. Herb was guessing outside and I came across the middle and Billy put it right on the money."

The 50-yard touchdown, Washington's second big play in 17 minutes, gave the Redskins a stunning 14-3 lead.

The Cowboys weren't finished, but the Redskins now had confidence to go with their intensity. Hill led Dallas downfield, but Hanburger tackled him for no gain on third-and-goal from the 2 and the Cowboys settled for Clark's 9-yard field goal. Six plays later, defensive tackle Jethro Pugh recovered Brown's fumble at the Dallas 46. Craig Morton's passes of 16 yards to receiver Gloster Richardson and 26 yards to receiver Bob Hayes put the Cowboys on the 6, but a holding penalty pushed them back and Clark narrowed the deficit to 14-9 with a 27-yarder.

Kilmer marched Washington 70 yards to the Dallas 15 to start the third quarter, but his subsequent third-down throw was picked off by linebacker Dave Edwards. However, Morton immediately fumbled at his 5. Petitbon recovered, but Washington's offense failed to take full advantage of the big break.

Brown was stopped for no gain by Cowboys tackle Bob Lilly and then dumped for a 5-yard loss by Edwards and middle linebacker Lee Roy Jordan. Kilmer was then sacked by Pugh and Cole for an 8-yard loss. Curt Knight's 25-yard field goal extended Washington's lead to 17-9.

As the quarter ended, a pair of passes from Kilmer to Taylor put the Redskins in scoring position again. This time, Knight hit from 32 yards.

"It was just garbage passes," Cole complained. "Kilmer threw timing over the middle. All the stuff our Flex defense couldn't handle. They were running the I-attack, and the Flex isn't as good against the I."

Since Morton hadn't been very good either–11-of-24 for 124 yards–Landry now replaced him with Roger Staubach, the scrambling hero of the Cowboys' 34-0 laugher the year before in Washington.

Staubach completed back-to-back passes of 28 and 25 yards to Hayes to reach the Redskins' 37. But after a pair of incompletions, Brundige chased down "Roger the Dodger" for a staggering 29-yard loss. It was a gigantic play because when Washington's offense couldn't produce a first down, Staubach led Dallas downfield again, hitting receiver Lance Alworth for 24 yards and tight end Mike Ditka for gains of 12, 16 and eight. Hill's 1-yard touchdown made it 20-16 with 3:08 remaining.

But Dallas would never get the ball back. Brown and Harraway had combined for 192 yards, but it was backup halfback Tommy Mason, another of Allen's "Ramskins," who bulled ahead for six on second-and-5 to enable Washington to run out the clock. The emotional Allen was so excited that he declined his usual milk to join his players for a beer on the plane ride home.

And when the Redskins arrived back at Dulles Airport, 5,000 delirious fans cheering "We're No. 1" and "Defense, Defense," were on hand to greet them.

"We could see all the cars from the air," Jefferson said. "It was just amazing. You can't really explain the feelings we had to see all those people and how much we meant to them."

And how much the victory meant to the Redskins, who would start the season 5-0 en route to their first playoff berth since 1945.

"That game made everyone realize that all George's talk about 'The Future is Now' wasn't just rhetoric," McDole said. "We were for real."

REDSKINS 20, COWBOYS 16

	1	2	3	4	TOTAL
REDSKINS	7	7	3	3	20
COWBOYS	0	9	0	7	16

◆ FIRST QUARTER
W – Harraway 57 run (Knight kick), W 7-0

◆ SECOND QUARTER
D – Clark 22 FG, W 7-3
W – Jefferson 50 pass from Kilmer (Knight kick), W 14-3
D – Clark 9 FG, W 14-6
D – Clark 27 FG, W 14-9

◆ THIRD QUARTER
W – Knight 25 FG, W 17-9

◆ FOURTH QUARTER
W – Knight 32 FG, W 20-9
D – Hill 1 run (Clark kick), W 20-16

photo by Ranny Routt

Washington receiver Charley Taylor eyes the pass that will clinch the 1972 NFC title as Dallas reserve cornerback Mark Washington dives in vain.

Dec. 31, 1972

Ring Out The Old

Redskins 26, Cowboys 3

The Dallas Cowboys had won the NFC title in 1970 before losing Super Bowl V to the Baltimore Colts on Jim O'Brien's last-second field goal. The Cowboys got back to the Super Bowl in 1971 and crushed the Miami Dolphins, 24-3.

So even though the Washington Redskins had rallied behind venerable quarterback Sonny Jurgensen to beat Dallas 24-20 on Oct. 22, 1972 at RFK Stadium, it was a confident bunch of Cowboys who arrived in Washington for the NFC Championship Game.

After all, the Cowboys had beaten the Redskins 34-24 at home just three weeks earlier. And thanks to backup quarterback Roger Staubach, they had scored two late touchdowns to win their playoff opener, 30-28, at San Francisco.

Staubach had been out almost all year with a separated shoulder, but now the man who had beaten Washington in 1970 and 1971 at RFK, was back in command. Dallas coach Tom Landry announced that Staubach would replace Craig Morton for the showdown with the Redskins.

"When we beat them in Dallas, we controlled the ball, ran the ball down their throats," said Cowboys running back Calvin Hill. "The thing we hadn't executed well against was their nickel [defense]. I don't know if we went in [to RFK] with the attitude of ramming it down their throats. It seemed like our entire game plan was to defeat the nickel. We must have changed our strategy three times that week, putting in elaborate substitution patterns. The last meeting, in Tom Landry's room the night before the game, we changed it again. Roger hadn't played all year. If were confused about how to attack the nickel, I'm sure he was too."

Meanwhile, the Redskins, coming off a 16-3 throttling of the Green Bay Packers in their first home playoff game since World War II, were being counted on to help heal a deeply racially divided city. Mayor Walter Washington visited Redskin Park before the Dallas game.

Defensive tackle Bill Brundige remembered the mayor saying, "You're the glue that's holding this city together. It doesn't matter if you're black, white, rich or poor, you're a Redskin fan. By winning, you have given every citizen in this city something special to have in common, pull together and root for you guys."

As if that responsibility weren't enough, the Redskins were battling the flu. Eleven players, including five starters, were sick as game day approached. But the Redskins, who had just four starters with championship rings, surely craved a title more than the ever-successful Cowboys. Washington had made the playoffs for the first time in 26 years in 1971, losing 24-20 at San Francisco, but that taste of postseason had just made the Redskins hungrier.

"Our goal was to get to the Super Bowl and win it," said Washington receiver Roy Jefferson. "It was a business-like atmosphere. We had the same players from the year before and now we all knew the system."

Redskins coach George Allen's "Over The Hill Gang," which included nine starters at least 30 years old, had flirted with a perfect season. Other than a 24-23 defeat at New England, Washington was unbeaten–despite losing Jurgensen with a torn Achilles' tendon–through 12 games. Then with the NFC East title clinched, Allen rested NFL rushing leader Larry Brown in the meaningless final losses to Dallas and Buffalo.

"We felt that if we all did what we were supposed to do, no one could beat us," said safety Brig Owens, whose career had begun on the Cowboys' taxi squad in 1965. "Everyone seemed to be so focused. We went the entire week with about one mistake in practice. Normally, there would be some going through the motions, but that week, you could hear the little 'pop' of guys getting ready with hard hits. We realized the opportunity we had."

That was especially true of quarterback Billy Kilmer, who had been given up on by San Francisco and New Orleans. Kilmer, who had replaced the injured Jurgensen for the second straight season, was having coffee early Sunday morning with teammates Len Hauss, Diron Talbert, Pat Fischer and Ron McDole when he read in the newspapers that Landry

33

had said the Cowboys would win because Staubach was the better athlete.

"That incensed me," Kilmer said. "I was ready to go right then."

Washington's title-starved fans were equally ready for the New Year's Eve battle for a berth in Super Bowl VII.

"Whenever we went into Washington, not only was the game intimidating but the fans inside the stadium and outside the stadium were intimidating," said Cowboys receiver Bob Hayes.

Allen ordered the public address announcer to introduce the Cowboys and then delay the introduction of the Redskins to allow the crowd's roar to build to unprecedented levels.

"You couldn't hear who was being introduced," said Hill, who later played for Allen's Redskins. "I'm sure it was a psychological ploy on George's part."

While the Cowboys were intimidated, the Redskins were reveling in the noise of perhaps RFK's loudest-ever throng.

"It was just an unbelievable feeling," Owens said. "The stadium was just rocking. You thought it was going to fall apart."

But as Jefferson said, "We were too excited when the game started. I was in the tunnel beforehand just trying to calm down."

The teams were scoreless into the second quarter when Washington's Curt Knight finished a 9:15 drive with an 18-yard field goal. Dallas, which had only gained 23 yards, again went nowhere. On Washington's subsequent third-and-10, Kilmer decided to test young cornerback Charlie Waters, whose superior play against the run had made him a starter ahead of ex-Green Bay star Herb Adderly. Kilmer's pass to receiver Charley Taylor went for 51 yards. Three plays later, Taylor caught a 15-yard slant for a touchdown and a 10-0 Washington lead.

The Cowboys finally came to life when feisty defensive tackle Talbert was penalized for roughing Staubach. The elusive quarterback then dashed for 29 yards to the Washington 32. Dallas settled for a

photo courtesy of the Washington Redskins

Redskins quarterback Billy Kilmer and George Allen teamed for a memorable New Year's Eve.

35-yard field goal by Toni Fritsch. Staubach's completions to receivers Lance Alworth and Ron Sellers set up Fritsch again as the half ended.

However, the kicker who had been perfect inside the 30 all season was wide left from 23 yards this time.

Late in the scoreless third quarter, Washington cornerback Mike Bass blunted Dallas' next scoring chance, brilliantly breaking up Staubach's bomb for the speedy Hayes.

"Mike was a very smart player with a lot of intensity," Hayes said. "He stayed back there like a weak safety and just read the play."

Washington's offense, which had managed only 22 yards since Taylor's touchdown, now finally began moving again. Kilmer's third-down throws to fullback Charley Harraway and Taylor ignited the drive. However, the Redskins soon faced another third-and-10. With Waters sidelined after breaking his arm on a punt return, Landry had inserted little-used youngster Mark Washington into the lineup instead of Adderly. Naturally, Kilmer looked Taylor's way again.

"I just told Charley to run as far as he could," said Kilmer, who was razor-sharp that afternoon, hitting 14-of-18 passes for 194 yards and two touchdowns. "I thought I had overthrown him. I don't know how he got to it. It was an electrifying moment."

Taylor's touchdown, with Washington diving at his heels, gave the Redskins a 17-3 advantage with just 14:12 to play.

The celebration only magnified when safety Roosevelt Taylor's hit on Hill five plays later forced a fumble which defensive end McDole recovered at the Dallas 38. Knight soon kicked a 39-yard field goal and when Brundige and end Verlon Biggs ruined the Cowboys' next series by sacking Staubach for a 10-yard loss, the usually erratic Knight extended the margin to 23-3 with a 46-yarder.

"Their defense shut us down," Staubach said. "We really just couldn't run. And we didn't do much in the passing game. I mean they just beat us."

Special teams ace Bob Brunet added to Dallas' misery by crunching Cliff Harris on the kickoff return.

"The crowd was stamping its feet, banging on the walls," Brundige said. "You could literally feel the sound cascading in your body."

Said Harraway, who had lost a championship game while with Cleveland, "It's hard to explain the feeling you get when you know you've won the game and it's still going on. It was just such a wonderful feeling. We beat Dallas and we were going to the Super Bowl."

Knight added the coup de grace with 76 seconds left, a 45-yarder to finalize the score at 26-3, Redskins.

"The Redskins played a perfect game," said Staubach, who passed for just 98 yards and was sacked three times while leading Dallas rushers with 59 yards.

"That was the beginning of the true bitter hatred that we felt toward each other," Waters said of the one-sided loss.

Allen, who had been 0-3 in the playoffs despite a 58-21-5 record during the seven previous regular seasons with the Los Angeles Rams and the Redskins, was finally a champion. His players carried him on their shoulders in the midst of the delirious fans who had stormed the field in the final seconds.

"It was nice to see George enjoying it," Jefferson said. "If I ever felt a coach deserved it, it was George. He wanted to win so much and he worked so hard. No team was ever better prepared than we were."

Allen was so excited after his biggest victory that instead of awarding a color television to the player of the game, he gave each one of the players a set.

"The championship game was like our Super Bowl which is part of the reason we didn't play well against Miami," McDole said.

The Redskins did lose the Super Bowl, 14-7, to the undefeated Dolphins and they wouldn't get back to the ultimate game for a decade, five years after Allen left town. But on that memorable New Year's Eve, Allen and his "Over The Hill Gang" were the kings of Capitol Hill and beyond.

REDSKINS 26, COWBOYS 3

	1	2	3	4	TOTAL
COWBOYS	0	3	0	0	3
REDSKINS	0	10	0	16	26

◆ SECOND QUARTER
W - Knight 18 FG, W 3-0
W - Taylor 15 pass from Kilmer (Knight kick), W 10-0
D - Fritsch 33 FG, W 10-3

◆ FOURTH QUARTER
W - Taylor 45 pass from Kilmer (Knight kick), W 17-3
W - Knight 39 FG, W 20-3
W - Knight 46 FG, W 23-3
W - Knight 45 FG, W 26-3

photo by Ranny Routt

Washington safety Ken Houston wraps up Dallas fullback Walt Garrison and the victory in an unforgettable last-minute collision.

Oct. 8, 1973

Goal-line Glory
Redskins 14, Cowboys 7

Washington safety Ken Houston burst into the Hall of Fame in 1986, launched to Canton in part by his play against Dallas. The native Texan feasted on this rivalry, driven, perhaps, by this thought:

"You did not want to come home [to Texas] having lost to the Cowboys."

Nor did you want to stay in Washington. So Houston did his best to ensure victory. For eight seasons with the Redskins, Houston pestered the Cowboys. He was Sitting Bull and they were his General Custer.

Time and again, even when others grabbed more headlines, no one scalped Dallas more than Houston.

In 1974, he returned a punt 58 yards for a touchdown, the only such play in his career, as the Redskins won, 28-21. Houston was not the regular punt returner — that job belonged to an injured Larry Jones.

A year later, Houston intercepted a Roger Staubach pass in overtime to set up the game-winning score in a 30-24 victory. And, in 1978, Houston picked off a pass in the end zone intended for receiver Drew Pearson to preserve a 9-5 win.

The next season, with Dallas on the 3-yard line just before halftime, Houston blitzed Staubach and knocked the ball loose. Houston had stifled another drive and Washington won again, 34-20.

Of course, some defeats were mixed in as well, though even then Houston played well. Yes he was good against other teams. But it didn't rival his play against the Cowboys.

Houston owns a framed photograph, hanging on a wall in his home, that shows him leaping high for an interception against Dallas.

"I don't know how I jumped that high or why I jumped that high," said Houston, whom the Redskins obtained in a trade for five Houston Oilers in the spring of 1973. "It seemed like when I played Dallas, I got on another level."

First came The Tackle.

Even now, someone reminds Houston of his famous hit two or three times a week. Not that he minds the attention. After all, he got the better of this last-second goal-line collision with Dallas fullback Walt Garrison, who never understood the fuss.

"People say, 'God, Kenny Houston tackled Walt Garrison,' " he said. "If I had never been tackled in my life, it would have been a big deal. But Kenny wasn't the first one to stop me. And Kenny was a big guy."

So, too, was Garrison. Perhaps he didn't realize how tough it was to stop a 6-foot, 205-pound steer-wrestling just-a-pinch-between-your-cheek-and-gums fullback from gaining a few inches.

But that's what the 6-3, 198-pound Houston did in this Monday Night game between 3-0 Dallas and 2-1 Washington. The Redskins' strong safety corralled Garrison on a fourth-and-goal pass from the 4-yard-line with 24 seconds to play and the Redskins leading, 14-7. Garrison, planted on the goal line, jumped for quarterback Craig Morton's pass. Morton's pump fake had ignited Houston's charge so he arrived with the ball and wrapped up Garrison.

Still, in this battle for first place, no one could tell what had happened. A hushed crowd of 54,314 stood and watched, anticipating the worst. Like viewers at an accident site, they feared seeing the carnage but couldn't turn away. Some of Houston's teammates figured Garrison would score and the game would end tied.

"It was just frozen in time," said Redskins defensive tackle Bill Brundige, who pressured Morton, jumped to block the pass, then turned and watched history unfold. "When [Garrison] jumped up, it seemed like he hung there forever. He caught the ball and everyone just stopped like, 'That's it.' "

Even Houston had his doubts.

"I thought [Garrison] was going to step in because I knew where he was," Houston said. "[Then] he was trying to lateral the ball and I was yelling for [safety] Brig [Owens] to help me. And it was like I was talking on the telephone. That's how quiet it was. I'll never forget that. It was like I was the only voice on the field and everyone else was holding their breath and waiting for it to happen. No one said a word. Then when everyone realized what had happened, it got louder and louder and louder."

Garrison scrapped any notion of scoring and lateralled the ball, which was smothered by Redskins near the 5.

Slight changes could have altered the outcome. Fortunately for Washington, Houston had read the play perfectly. Dallas had run a similar play earlier in the game and Houston remembered that in the huddle. When linebacker Chris Hanburger called the defense, Houston spoke up.

"Call another," he told Hanburger, who did just that. In the new alignment, Houston and Owens played a combination coverage on the tight end and running back. Garrison ran a circle route, coming from the strong side and running inside the linebacker. The tight end, Jean Fugett, is supposed to go outside.

In Dallas' thinking, Houston would pick up Fugett. But when Fugett, the first option, released, Houston stood his ground, waiting for Garrison. And Owens covered Fugett.

Or, at least, was supposed to. Fugett said that didn't happen.

"I was wide open," Fugett recalled. "If Brig was coming to get me, he was a long way away. If [Morton] had done a read, I would have gotten the ball. I was supposed to be the first read, but rather than take a chance on a young tight end, you go with the veteran fullback who could bull his way in."

Except that Fugett didn't think Garrison could do that. Not this time.

"The circle pass is a difficult pass for a quarterback to lead," Fugett said. "You have to throw it right to the receiver, you can't lead him. A receiver usually has to slow down and catch it so they don't have that momentum. When Walt slowed down to catch it and I saw Kenny beeline to him, I knew there was no way he'd get in. His momentum was stopped."

Dallas running back Calvin Hill said, "Garrison just didn't have a chance. So it looked a lot better than it was. It wasn't Earl Campbell and Jack Tatum on the goal line."

But when Houston broke on the ball, he intended to pick it off and race for a touchdown. He'd already had an NFL-record nine of those in his career — all with the Oilers.

But Houston didn't arrive in time for the interception. Instead he made the Redskins' most famous tackle. It helped that Houston reached Garrison while the Dallas back was still in the air.

"If he had the ball and got both feet on the ground, it would have been a tossup," Houston said. "I would have to hit him hard enough to knock him back and that's very difficult. I would probably be able to do that two out of 10 times."

Washington defensive tackle Diron Talbert said, "That may be the defensive play of the century."

That's why Houston is asked about the play so often. He even said Garrison requested a picture of the famous play.

"It made my name more recognizable every time the Redskins played," said Garrison, who retired in 1974 with 3,886 yards rushing and another 1,794 receiving. "It seemed some sportscaster would bring it up. But that was OK."

Neither team played OK early. But with 49 seconds remaining in the first half, Dallas quarterback Roger Staubach snapped the scoreless tie, tossing a 15-yard touchdown pass to receiver Otto Stowe. The 16-play drive was aided by three penalties, including a roughing-the-punter flag on Bill Malinchak.

But Washington quarterback Sonny Jurgensen answered quickly, moving the Redskins into position for a 44-yard Curt Knight field goal attempt. Knight, however, continued his season-long slump and missed the kick as time expired.

Dallas' first-half domination wasn't reflected in its 7-0 halftime lead. The Cowboys recorded 13 first downs to the Redskins' three. But Washington's special teams, despite the penalty, kept the game close. Redskins coach George Allen showed foresight by having the special teams introduced before the game rather than the offense or defense.

Malinchak was announced first and that, too, was prophetic. In the first quarter, Malinchak was switched from an outside rusher to the inside. He ripped through the middle and blocked Marv Bateman's punt. But the Redskins squandered the opportunity when Knight's 53-yard try was blocked by Pat Toomay.

Dallas attempted a field goal on its next possession, but Verlon Biggs and Ron McDole blocked Toni Fritsch's kick.

Despite the Cowboys' success moving the ball, coach Tom Landry switched quarterbacks. Supposedly, Staubach had suffered a charley horse.

"I was livid," Staubach remembered. "He mentioned that I was hurt. Oh, I had a bruise, but nothing to be taken out of the game for."

It meant no redemption from the 1972 NFC Championship Game for Staubach, who termed his play in that 26-3 loss "embarrassing." That game haunted Staubach, who had used it as offseason motivation, as had his teammates. In Dallas' practice facility locker room hung a burgundy Redskin-helmet plaque with the inscription: "Washington Redskins: 1972 NFC champions."

For a change, the Cowboys chased the Redskins. Before the rematch, one anonymous Cowboy said, "We think about the Redskins every day."

On this day Dallas was in command, despite the narrow lead. Washington's offense had mustered nothing except frustration. Jurgensen was making only his second start since his torn Achilles' tendon 11 months earlier. And running back Larry Brown, who had rushed for more than 4,000 yards in the previous four seasons, had gained just 130 in the season's first three games.

Knight's misses from 53, 44 and 30 yards didn't help. A Pro Bowler two years earlier, Knight was slumping badly enough that Allen eschewed a field goal on fourth-and-inches from the 10 early in the fourth quarter. Dallas stuffed fullback Charley Harraway for no gain.

Eventually, Washington managed a scoring drive. Jurgensen completed four passes — two to favorite receiver Charley Taylor for 24 yards — pushing the ball to the Dallas 18. Then Taylor took advantage of cornerback Charlie Waters, another Cowboy seeking atonement as well for the championship game.

Waters broke his shoulder in that loss and rebroke it again two more times over the next month. He was hospitalized for two months and in pain for four. Doubt existed over Waters' NFL future. But he had returned and this time had held the NFC's leading receiver in check.

But, with the ball on the 18, Jurgensen called for Taylor to run a post pattern. After Taylor made his break in the end zone, Waters grabbed his shirt, drawing an interference penalty and placing the ball on the 1. Jurgensen hit Taylor, beating Waters on a square-out, for the tying score with 3:39 remaining.

The tie lasted three plays.

On Dallas' next series, Morton dropped back to pass on third-and-9 at the Cowboys' 19. Under intense pressure, he spotted tight end Billy Joe DuPree in the right flat, but Owens read the play. He raced in front of DuPree, grabbed

the pass and ran 26 yards untouched, snapping the tie.

With 1:52 left, Dallas' hopes diminished greatly as Bateman punted again. But the Cowboys caught a break when the ball bounced off the back of the Redskins' Jerry Smith and Dallas recovered at the 27.

The Cowboys reached the 4 in five plays, the last of which was a 17-yard Morton to Garrison pass on fourth-and-1.

After three incomplete passes, Houston made his fateful play to end this defensive gem.

"That was a pure shock," said Dallas center John Fitzgerald. "We weren't at the point where we thought just because we were at the goal line we were going to score for sure. But when Walt caught the ball . . . Kenny Houston held him up and then, all of a sudden, all hell broke loose."

Dallas outgained Washington 269-174 and ran 25 more plays; Hill, the NFC's leading rusher, gained 103 yards while Brown was held to 36. Somehow, the Redskins won. Somehow, Houston stopped Garrison.

"Every play in the game was like a civil war," Allen said afterward. "Every play we gave a little more blood. Every play meant the game."

Especially the last one.

The Redskins went on to finish 10-4 and lost at Minnesota in the first round of the playoffs. Dallas, which got revenge with a 27-7 win Dec. 9, ended with the same record and also lost to Minnesota, but not until the NFC Championship.

As for Houston, he led the team in interceptions with six and was named to the Pro Bowl. For Redskins fans his tackle alone should have earned him a berth.

"It was one of those classic mano a mano confrontations," Brundige said. "Houston and Garrison. And Kenny got him."

REDSKINS 14, COWBOYS 7

	1	2	3	4	TOTAL
COWBOYS	0	7	0	0	7
REDSKINS	0	0	0	14	14

◆ **SECOND QUARTER**
D - Stowe 15 pass from Staubach (Fritsch kick), D 7-0

◆ **FOURTH QUARTER**
W - Taylor 1 pass from Jurgensen (Knight kick), 7-7
W - Owens 26 interception return (Knight kick), W 14-7

George Allen

When George Allen arrived in Washington in 1971 to become coach and general manager of the Redskins, the Dallas Cowboys were the defending NFC champions. They had won five straight conference or division titles. The Redskins hadn't been to the playoffs since 1945.

Allen, who had been a winner with the Los Angeles Rams except at playoff time, was determined to erase that blot from his resume. The Cowboys stood in his way. So he hated Dallas. Everything about Dallas. When the Redskins drafted defensive end Dallas Hickman in 1975, Allen wouldn't call him by his first name.

"To George, beating Dallas was a mission," said Redskins general manager Charley Casserly, a one-time Allen intern.

Allen's need to conquer the Cowboys became Ahab-like and Dallas coach Tom Landry was his white whale.

Before the 1972 NFC Championship Game against Dallas, Allen told his players, "If I could do this, it would just be me and Tom Landry at the 50 duking it out if that meant the game."

As well-respected former defensive coordinators, Allen and Landry had much in common. But for the emotional Allen, the stoic Landry and the Cowboys were the NFL's pampered favorites while the league was out to get him and his bad-boy Redskins.

"George used to call Tom Landry during the week of the game and ask how his team was," said Redskins defensive tackle Diron Talbert. "We'd be sitting in the jacuzzi and George would come in, get in a crouch and say, 'We're gonna get that [Cowboys quarterback Roger] Staubach and wring his neck!' George would get crazy during Dallas week."

And that was before the game. But all the pep rally-type signs and "Beat Dallas" T-shirts at Redskin Park and Allen's redoubled nervous habits of tugging the bill of his cap and licking his fingers paled in comparison to his postgame moods.

Allen was never happier than after that 1972 Championship Game victory over Dallas and never lower than after one of his eight losses in 15 meetings with the Cowboys.

In 1974, Dallas rookie backup quarterback Clint Longley stunned the Redskins with a last-minute, game-winning touchdown pass to receiver Drew Pearson. Allen — who had already lost six playoff games — called it "probably the toughest loss I've ever had."

Allen never coached another NFL game after leaving the Redskins. His last connection to the league came through the Cowboys, of all clubs. Allen was a color commentator on Dallas' preseason games in 1988, two years before his death.

"When I went into the Hall of Fame of the Washington Touchdown Club, George sat down beside me," Landry recalled. "He didn't even say hello. He said, 'I know it. Drew Pearson broke his route. That's the reason you were able to beat us.' "

photo courtesy of the Washington Redskins

Tom Landry

There was Tom Landry, sitting on this darn horse, dressed up as a cowboy – a real cowboy – complete with hat, scarf, long coat, chaps and boots. Yes, the same stoic Tom Landry, the one whose stone face on the sideline had become his trademark as much as the fedora he wore.

But this had nothing to do with football. This was the other side of Tom Landry rarely seen, and especially not in Washington or during Redskins Week when the Cowboys were preparing to play what had become more than a football game during the 1970s and early 1980s. This was Landry letting what little hair he still had down, filming an American Express commercial that began airing nationwide in 1982.

"I didn't expect that script," said Landry, who initially turned down the offer but changed his mind during the 1982 players' strike when he had some extra time on his hands. "I expected the 'No one knows me without my hat,' that's what I thought it was going to be."

But even the people at American Express recognized the popularity of the Cowboys-Redskins' rivalry that had swept through the nation. The ad folks couldn't resist, changing their signature line to accommodate what was hot. Instead, the commercial had Landry walking into this saloon, suddenly surrounded not by Indians, but by football-clad Redskins. And he says, "You never know when you're going to be surrounded by Redskins."

This is about as funny as the Redskins' rivalry ever was for Landry, who became obsessed with beating Washington once George Allen arrived in 1971. During Landry's 29 seasons, his record against the Redskins was 32-24-2. Against Allen, it was 8-7, including that 26-3 loss in the 1972 NFC championship, the only time they met during the playoffs. Landry's record against Gibbs was 8-8, including a

photo courtesy of the Dallas Cowboys

31-17 loss to Washington in the 1982 NFC title game.

And how appropriate was it that Landry's final victory came against the Redskins, 24-17, in Game 15 of the 1988 season?

Now, when Landry looks back at those days, spiced by Allen's pre-game mental gymnastics and unending desire to gain a competitive edge, he says, "Ol' George, he was always the psychologist."

But Landry's players detected a significant edge to Landry the week of the Redskins games.

"I think it got to Tom, it really did," said free safety Cliff Harris of the running feud with the Redskins and Allen. "It bothered Tom. Now I thought it was all humorous. I loved it. It was great. Tom would never show it publicly or comment on it, but you could tell it would upset him at times. He wanted to beat them."

Landry's 29-year career with Dallas spanned eight coaches in Washington, beginning with Mike Nixon in 1960, the Cowboys' first year of the existence, and lasting through Bill McPeak, Otto Graham, Vince Lombardi, Bill Austin, Allen, Jack Pardee and finally Gibbs. And while Landry never really openly contributed to the shenanigans these two franchises engaged in twice yearly, he never stopped his players from participating.

Maybe he lived the rivalry vicariously through them, especially during Allen's 1971-77 reign.

"That was the real rivalry," Landry said of facing the Redskins with Allen. "Once George got out of there it was different. When Joe Gibbs came in – I love Joe Gibbs, he's a great friend of mine – we kind of lost the real excitement of the game, although it was still pretty exciting.

"But it wasn't like it was when George was there."

No, not even for this Cowboy.

Cowboys running back Calvin Hill rips through an opening in the Redskins' defense. Hill found many holes to run through in this 1973 game.

Dec. 9, 1973

Getting Even

Cowboys 27, Redskins 7

The Cowboys-Redskins rivalry began as a front office thing, the two owners, Washington's George Preston Marshall and Dallas' Clint Murchison, butting heads at seemingly every pass.

The landscape of the country's political arena in those early years sprayed some antagonistic fuel on this combustible combination, those brash Texans infiltrating hoity-toity Redskins country on the coattails of Texas-bred Vice President and then President Lyndon Baines Johnson during the first eight years of the Cowboys' existence .

But by 1973, these outside forces had become merely ancillary. This had become real-life Cowboys and Indians, played out on a 100-yard piece of land by two teams that, well, just didn't like each other.

"There always will be animosity between these two teams," said Cowboys Hall of Famer Lee Roy Jordan. "Especially when they are trying to take your title, your position and your money."

By golly, the Redskins had done all that to the Cowboys. This competitive pirating began with the arrival of coach George Allen in Washington in 1971. The Redskins had interrupted six consecutive losses to the Cowboys with a 20-16 victory at the Cotton Bowl in Allen's first Washington meeting with Dallas. Consider that an opening salvo, though it was just one game as the Cowboys went on to win their first Super Bowl that season.

But in 1972, the Redskins torpedoed the Cowboys' dominance, not only edging them by one game for their first Eastern Division title since 1945, but cold-cocking Dallas in the NFC Championship Game. And those mean, old Redskins were going to the Super Bowl, the yearly affair the Cowboys thought had become their inalienable right to attend after two consecutive appearances.

And if all that were not instigating enough, Washington knocked Dallas off its high horse again the first meeting in 1973, beating them 14-7 at RFK in the fourth game of the season when Washington's Ken Houston made his legendary tackle of Cowboys rough-and-tumble fullback Walt Garrison just

outside the goal line on the game's final play. Man, these Texans were seething.

That's humidity you find throughout the state of Texas, not humility.

Plus, wouldn't you know it, this 13th game of 1973 had the makings of a good, old-fashioned showdown with the division title at stake. Washington led the NFC East at 9-3 after 12 games, having to finish the season playing Dallas and Philadelphia. Dallas was second at 8-4, finishing with Washington and St. Louis. The Cowboys didn't need to just beat the Redskins, that having become an increasingly difficult chore by now, but they had to beat them by more than seven points to gain a tie-breaker advantage over Washington.

So there was blood pumping in Dallas that Sunday afternoon.

"This is probably one of the most important games that we've played, in many, many years, and I even put the Super Bowl in that," said Cowboys president Tex Schramm at the time.

At stake was far more than a division title. This was about honor and a way of football for these helmeted Hatfields and McCoys. All the stops were being pulled out. The Cowboys lifted the no-banner rule at Texas Stadium, a cue for the high-brow Texans who monopolized the high-priced seats at the new stadium to let their hair down this once. Quarterback Roger Staubach and Allen traded verbal shots, the media and Redskins defensive tackle Diron Talbert more than willing to serve as conduits. And before it was all over, there was Dallas, insisting Allen had instructed his defenders to bark out offensive-like signals to cause the Cowboys to jump offsides, which, of course, Allen later would call "ridiculous."

Kids' stuff. Good stuff.

Allen, in just two seasons, had figured out how to get under Staubach's skin, maybe the best way to gain a competitive edge on the fiery Naval Academy graduate and 1963 Heisman Trophy winner who took everything to heart. And Allen's sidekick in agitating, Talbert, further stoked these flames, saying the Cowboys would have been better off in

"Yeah, we really rubbed it in," Cowboys center John Fitzgerald said, still taking a measure of pleasure from the memory. "That must have chafed George's [butt] real good."

that 1972 championship game had they started Craig Morton at quarterback instead of Staubach.

Might as well have called the Vietnam vet a communist.

"That is also when we started adapting defenses to stop them," Cowboys corner Charlie Waters said. "We started concentrating on them a little bit more instead of them just concentrating on us. We paid a little more attention to them."

Certainly it didn't hurt their cause that Washington quarterback Billy Kilmer had been hospitalized all week with a stomach disorder, forcing Allen to start 39-year-old Sonny Jurgensen. Because the Cowboys' defense did a number on the Redskins, forcing three turnovers, recording three sacks and limiting them to just 155 total yards – 46 in the second half – in the 27-7 victory, "one of those satisfying wins," said Cowboys defensive end Larry Cole, who predicted before the game that Dallas would win by 20 if it played well.

"A key game, giving us a chance to win the division title, and especially after losing the '72 championship game to them," Staubach said.

But ask the Redskins. They let this one get away, they'll say. And with good reason. Why kicker Curt Knight missed three second-quarter field goals; one from 23 yards, another from 28 yards after Houston had recovered a Staubach fumble at the Washington 30 and again from 37 yards just for good measure as the half ended, rendering Jurgensen's 32-yard drive in 18 seconds insignificant.

And to think Knight had been perfect from less than 30 yards going into that game.

But despite all those misses, the Redskins trailed only 3-0 at halftime. The Cowboys had turned a Jurgensen fumble forced by this rookie defensive end Harvey Martin and recovered by linebacker Rodrigo Barnes into a 9-yard Toni Fritsch field goal with 29 seconds remaining.

"It's hard to generate a lot of offense when you have a few dropped balls and a couple of bad kicks," Washington receiver Charley Taylor re-

membered. "We had breakdowns all over the place. And I remember that being the noisiest game in Texas that I ever played in. Normally they're not vocal, but it seemed like the fans were coming over the PA system."

Matters grew considerably worse for the Redskins in the second half. Fullback Charley Harraway's fumble, forced by free safety Cliff Harris and recovered by cornerback Mel Renfro at the Washington 39, led to Dallas' first touchdown. That was a painful 6-yard run by Staubach for the 10-0 lead midway through the third quarter.

"[Washington middle linebacker] Harold McLinton gave me a real dirty shot as I scored on a quarterback draw, and broke my ribs," Staubach said. "I wore rib pads after that game. I remember after the game we had a party over at Clint Murchison's. I was over there with these broken ribs, and I never felt so good in my life after beating the Redskins."

Still, the beating did not become decisive until late in the third quarter when the Cowboys drove 70 yards to score on running back Calvin Hill's 1-yard run, stretching their lead to 17-0. A 31-yard Staubach-to-Bob Hayes completion was the impetus for the touchdown.

"I don't know how he caught it, I went right over the ball," insisted Washington cornerback Pat Fischer of the second-and-eight play from the Cowboys' 32. "Staubach rolled out and Hayes ran an out. I realized I was a half-step late so I dove out for the ball. I don't know how he even saw the ball."

"Bullet Bob" saw the ball all right, then Garrison accounted for the next 30 yards, running for 10 and catching two balls for 20 to set up the Cowboys, first-and-goal at the 7. Hill did the rest, covering the needed seven yards in three plays, and as it turned out, giving Dallas its needed margin of victory to eventually win a tie-breaker with Washington for the division title.

If that had not been clue enough that the Redskins were about to abdicate their brief reign, the Cowboys drove the point home in the fourth quarter when Staubach engineered two drives worth 10 more points to take a 27-0 lead. Only then were the Redskins able to score. Linebacker Dave Robinson blocked Marv Bateman's punt, which Ken Stone recovered at the 12 and ran it in for the touchdown.

But Hill had done far too much damage on the ground, rushing for 110 yards and going over the 1,000-yard mark for the second consecutive season. The Cowboys, as a team, rushed for 193 yards behind the offensive line of center John Fitzgerald, tackles Rayfield Wright and Ralph Neeley, and guards Blaine Nye and John Niland. And Jurgensen had done far too little, passing for only 114 yards, and none of his 11 completions gaining more than 22 yards.

So with only 3:32 remaining, there would be no breathless Jurgensen comeback this time. In fact, Dallas unmercifully ground out every one of those seconds after recovering an onside kick, marching down to the Washington 2. There, with less than 20 seconds remaining and Washington unable to stop the clock, the Cowboys simply turned their backs on the visitors and walked away, leaving the ball, the Redskins and their previous frustrations at the goal line.

"It was fitting to leave the ball there, and let them stare at it," Cole would say, unintentionally calibrating the depth of this rivalry.

"Yeah, we really rubbed it in," Cowboys center John Fitzgerald said, still taking a measure of pleasure from the memory. "That must have chafed George's [butt] real good."

And the flamboyant Martin said he is sure of one thing: "I was talking a lot of noise. And being a rookie, it must have been big noise."

The game rendered huge ramifications. Both teams would win their final game to finish 10-4, tying for the NFC East title. But remember that tie-breaker. The Cowboys had beaten the Redskins by more than seven points. By 20 to be exact, meaning Dallas won the division crown by 13 points, outscoring Washington 34-21 in the two-game series.

"I didn't know what I was doing, but I knew we were real excited because we had an opportunity to go to the play-offs, and do it the right way by winning the East," Martin said. "All we had to do was beat the Redskins, and because

the Redskins had beaten us on Monday night we were ready."

The Cowboys went on to win their first-round playoff game, beating the Los Angeles Rams, 27-16. The wild-card Redskins went nowhere, losing to Minnesota, 27-20. And though the Cowboys lost to the Vikings, 27-10, the following week, at least they had regained the division title and had returned to the NFC Championship Game.

Maybe even more gratifying at this point of the blood-pumping feud, the second-place, wild-card Redskins were back home watching, even though they would proclaim themselves division "co-champions" on the cover of their 1974 media guide.

"Losing to Dallas was the worst feeling in the world," Talbert said. "You'd rather have your arm cut off."

And the feelings were a two-way nerve, Cowboys defensive end Pat Toomay having said after this latest triumph, "A perfect victory is beating Washington and George Allen."

So balance had been restored to this rivalry, the pendulum doing a 180, now allowing these insufferable Texans to regain their bragging rights.

"The Cowboys had been walking through the NFC East, and all of a sudden here come the Redskins," rationalizes wide receiver Drew Pearson, a rookie that 1973 season. "So now we've got to fight these guys every year for the title, and because of that it upsets the dominance that Dallas once had in the NFC East.

"And with two teams vying for the top spot, and especially when you play twice a year, it's almost natural a rivalry is going to break out."

Son, had it ever.

COWBOYS 27, REDSKINS 7

	1	2	3	4	TOTAL
REDSKINS	0	0	0	7	7
COWBOYS	0	3	14	10	27

◆ SECOND QUARTER
D - Fritsch 9 FG, D 3-0

◆ THIRD QUARTER
D - Staubach 5 run (Fritsch kick), D 10-0
D - Hill 1 run (Fritsch kick), D 17-0

◆ FOURTH QUARTER
D - Hill 2 run (Fritsch kick), Cowboys, D 24-0
D - Fritsch 27 FG, D 27-0
W - Stone 12 return of blocked punt (Knight kick), D 27-7

Cowboys quarterback Clint Longley didn't have much of an NFL career. But one game, and pass, forever made him a household name in Dallas and Washington.

Nov. 28, 1974

Longley Shot
Cowboys 24, Redskins 23

The star quarterbacks of the team with the blue star on its helmets have had everyday names like Roger or golden ones like Troy. The Dallas Cowboys haven't been led by a passer with a good ol' Texas name like Billy Bob or Butch.

With one exception. And boy was Clint Longley exceptional, especially on Thanksgiving Day 1974.

That summer Longley may have been joining the haughty Cowboys, who had reached four straight NFC championship games. But the raw newcomer, who had walked on at tiny Abilene Christian, never acted like your typical lowly rookie.

"Clint was a throwback," said Cowboys center John Fitzgerald. "He'd have a shooting gallery in his room at training camp. He'd have a sandbag, a pillow, a holster, a pistol and a rifle in there. And he'd go hunting rattlesnakes."

Receiver Drew Pearson remembered Longley shooting rabbits from the dormitory window. But Longley wasn't just letting off steam during a grueling and tedious training camp. He was always, well, a little different.

"An exciting afternoon for Clint was to drive the [Interstate] 635 loop and see how fast he could get around," Pearson said.

Then there was the pony.

"We were living at a place that had a little spread and Clint called and said he had to get rid of this little pony and wanted to know if I wanted it," recalled Dallas safety Charlie Waters. "So he brings it over. Clint had taken the backseat out of his Cadillac and the pony's head is sticking out the window. Unbelievable. Only Clint would do this."

Longley had to be colorful to attract any attention in 1974. Roger Staubach and Craig Morton, each of whom had quarterbacked the Cowboys to the Super Bowl, were ahead of the rookie on the depth chart. Longley would chart the plays on game days. However, there was some question whether he even knew them.

"Clint used to sit with me on the plane, but he didn't study," Staubach said. "Clint had ability, but he didn't work at it. He didn't even know the formations."

Longley's life began to change on Oct. 22 after the Cowboys ended the five-plus year duel between Staubach and Morton by trading the latter to the New York Giants. Longley was now one play away from guiding America's Team.

Longley may not have taken a snap in a game, but he had proven he had a NFL arm in practice.

"We knew what Clint had as far as an ability to throw a rocket and look off defenders because he was the quarterback who went against us all the time," Waters said.

Safety Cliff Harris said Longley's teammates pulled muscles trying to reach his overthrows. No wonder Longley was soon dubbed "The Mad Bomber."

Bombing was what the Cowboys seemed to be doing in 1974. They hadn't missed the playoffs since 1965, but their prospects of extending that streak looked bleak after four straight losses by a total of 16 points left Dallas at 1-4.

The Cowboys righted themselves and won six of their next seven, but the loss had come in Washington. Afterwards, always-blunt Redskins defensive tackle Diron Talbert vowed to knock the pesky Staubach out of the Thanskgiving rematch in Dallas.

"If you can knock Staubach out, you've got that rookie facing you," said Talbert, whose 8-3 Redskins needed just one victory to clinch their fourth straight playoff berth. "That's one of our goals. If we can do that, it's great. He [Staubach] is all they have."

But Dallas got on the board first on the balmy Texas afternoon. Halfback Robert Newhouse was the workhorse as the Cowboys reached the Washington 2 in 11 plays. However, an illegal procedure penalty and three incompletions — the last off tight end Billy Joe DuPree's fingertips — forced Dallas to settle for a 24-yard field goal by Efren Herrera.

The Redskins responded with a 67-yard field goal drive. Quarterback Billy Kilmer's 16-yard pass to tight end Jerry Smith and an 11-yard run by fullback Moses Denson set up Mark Moseley's 45-yard kick.

When linebacker Dave Robinson ended Dallas' next series by intercepting Staubach's pass for DuPree and rumbling 29 yards to the Dallas 23, Moseley soon followed with a 34-yard field goal.

Talbert – playing on an ailing right knee – sacked Staubach for losses on consecutive plays late in the second quarter, but Washington failed to take ad-

"One of those angels was sitting on Clint's shoulder," Schramm said. "We knew he could throw the ball, but nobody dreamed [this] and as it turned out, he couldn't do it again."

vantage of a subsequent 58-yard march when Moseley's 50-yarder was short. However, Cowboys fullback Walt Garrison fumbled on the next play. Talbert recovered at the Dallas 32 with 11 seconds left. Moseley's 39-yard field goal gave the Redskins a 9-3 halftime lead.

Garrison lost another fumble to start the third quarter. Robinson recovered at the Dallas 39 and seven plays later, Kilmer hit ex-Cowboys halfback Duane Thomas for the 9-yard touchdown pass.

On second-and-7 from the Dallas 44, Staubach scrambled for nine yards, but suffered a game-ending concussion on Robinson's tackle. Cowboys coach Tom Landry, who had contemplated pulling the ineffective Staubach (3-for-11, 32 yards) earlier, now had no choice but to insert the untested Longley.

"Clint's eyes were as big as half dollars," said Dallas receiver Bob Hayes.

"I had to find my helmet first," said Longley, who admitted to being a little scared about making his NFL debut in this situation on national television. "I know how the Redskins must have felt when I went in."

They felt they had made the playoffs.

"I thought the game was over when we knocked Staubach out," said Redskins backup safety Ken Stone.

It wasn't. After handing off to Newhouse and missing him on a screen, Longley passed to Garrison for 10 yards. Two plays later, Longley hit DuPree for the 35-yard touchdown. The Cowboys were now Longley's.

"I brought in a play and was explaining it to Clint," Garrison recalled. "I got it wrong just a little at one point and he says, 'Shut up. I know the plays!' So I shut up."

When the Cowboys got the ball back, Longley marched them 70 yards in 10 plays with Garrison scoring from the 1 to put Dallas on top, 17-16, with 1:16 left in the quarter.

"Clint just went back there and winged it," said

Dallas defensive end Larry Cole. "It was sandlot football. That's why he was successful. They expected him to read all these keys and he didn't do it."

The Redskins quickly regained the lead as Kilmer connected on a 38-yard pass to receiver Roy Jefferson and Thomas then followed Smith's block and raced 19 yards. Washington led 23-17 with 13:26 remaining.

Cowboys tight end Charles Young fumbled the ball right back to Washington at the Dallas 16, but Redskins offensive coordinator Ted Marchibroda called three running plays. The decision not to go for the kill backfired when Ed "Too Tall" Jones blocked Moseley's 24-yard field goal try.

"It was a chip shot," Kilmer said. "Moseley was a good kicker. He just mis-hit the ball and didn't get it over the line of scrimmage. If he made the field goal, their last drive wouldn't have mattered."

When Pearson lost Dallas' fourth fumble of the day with 2:32 to go, the Cowboys' playoff hopes appeared dead.

"We had that thing wrapped up," recalled Redskins receiver Charley Taylor. "We could just about smell the turkey on the plane."

But Marchibroda, following coach George Allen's conservative nature, again ordered Kilmer to hand off three times. After Mike Bragg's punt, Longley had one last shot at his own 40 with no timeouts and 1:45 left.

Longley's fourth-and-6 throw to Hayes gained just enough for the first down as the Redskins complained to the officials in vain about the spot. Longley missed Pearson on the next play. Dallas was at midfield with 35 seconds left. Landry called for a 20-yard in route, but Pearson and Longley had other ideas.

"I told Clint I was going to run a turn-in and take off," Pearson said. "Clint said, 'Fine. Go deep.'"

Across the line, Stone and veteran cornerback Mike Bass were supposed to cover Pearson with a

The Cowboys are 20-8-1 on Thanksgiving and have played at home every Turkey Day since 1966, except for 1975 and 1977 when they did not participate in the Thursday game. Dallas has faced Washington more than any other opponent on Thanksgiving, winning all five meetings by an average margin of 12 points.

> *"I saw Stone stop and Pearson run right past him," Jefferson said. "I was saying, 'No. No. No. I can't believe it!' "*

double zone.

"We had the best defense for what they did, it's just that they beat the defense," said linebacker Chris Hanburger, who called Washington's defensive signals.

"I had the inside and Mike had the outside," Stone said. "Drew gave a quick cut to the inside. We both bit. I was the rookie, so I got blamed."

Said Pearson, "With nobody on my head, I got a free release off the line and was able to get downfield pretty quickly. I gave Stone the inside fake and Bass, on the outside, was never a factor, Stone bit hard on the in route because that was a big play for us."

But never this big. Longley's pass was perfect. Pearson raced into the end zone untouched. Cowboys 24, Redskins 23.

"I saw Stone stop and Pearson run right past him," Jefferson said. "I was saying, 'No. No. No. I can't believe it!' "

Neither could the Texas Stadium crowd which erupted with joy after the highest point of a downbeat season which wound up with Dallas missing the playoffs for the first time in nine years.

"I remember it was loud coming off the field, the crowd noise was ringing in the earholes of my helmet," Stone said.

"That's one of those games that happens only once in a lifetime," said Cowboys president Tex Schramm, who had given Cincinnati a fifth-round draft pick for Longley that spring.

That didn't make the bitter defeat any easier for the Redskins to take.

"I can't remember a more disappointing loss," said Allen of the defeat which would cost Washington the NFC East title and homefield advantage in the playoffs from which they were eliminated in the first round by the Los Angeles Rams.

Talbert, swarmed by the media, was asked about Longley and said he didn't know who he was. "He was pretty damn good," Talbert said when informed of Longley's identity.

"One of those angels was sitting on Clint's shoulder," Schramm said. "We knew he could throw the ball, but nobody

dreamed [this] and as it turned out, he couldn't do it again."

Longley's poor work habits and attitude would cost him.

After backing up Staubach for the rest of 1974 and 1975, Longley came to training camp in 1976 in a battle with rookie Danny White. Maybe the pressure got to him. Maybe he was just being his unpredictable self. But one day in practice, Longley cursed out Pearson when he dropped a pass. Staubach got mad at Longley and when the workout was over, they went to an adjacent baseball field to settle their differences. Longley got in the first shot before Staubach wrestled him to the ground.

Assistant coach Dan Reeves broke up the fight, but three days later just before camp ended, Longley and Staubach were virtually alone in the locker room. Staubach was looking down when Longley suddenly punched him and briefly knocked him senseless. While Staubach was taken for stitches, Longley hitched a ride to the airport and was soon an ex-Cowboy.

Longley signed with San Diego and started one game for the Chargers that year. His career ended when St. Louis cut him in the summer of 1978 and he quickly faded back into obscurity.

But as Cowboys guard Blaine Nye said, on Thanksgiving Day 1974, Longley produced the memorable "victory of the uncluttered mind."

COWBOYS 24, REDSKINS 23

	1	2	3	4	TOTAL
REDSKINS	3	6	7	7	23
COWBOYS	3	0	14	7	24

◆ **FIRST QUARTER**
D - Herrera 24 FG, D 3-0
W - Moseley 45 FG, W 3-3

◆ **SECOND QUARTER**
W - Moseley 34 FG, W 6-3
W - Moseley 39 FG, W 9-3

◆ **THIRD QUARTER**
W - Thomas 9 pass from Kilmer (Moseley kick), W 16-3
D - DuPree 35 pass from Longley (Herrera kick), W 16-10
D - Garrison 1 run (Herrera kick), D 17-16

◆ **FOURTH QUARTER**
W - Thomas 19 run (Moseley kick), W 23-17
D - Pearson 50 pass from Longley (Herrera kick), D 24-23

photo courtesy of Washington Redskins

Redskins quarterback Billy Kilmer was often down, but never out as the Cowboys often learned.

Nov. 2, 1975

Working Overtime

Redskins 30, Cowboys 24

Billy Kilmer, doubled over and eyeing his blood-stained pants, clutched the sides of his helmet in anger. Then he trotted off the field as Washington's fans showered the Redskins' quarterback with boos.

On the Dallas sideline, safety Cliff Harris celebrated the only interception return for a touchdown in his 10-year career.

With 5:03 to play — and Dallas leading by a touchdown — RFK Stadium's 55,004 fans braced for another crushing loss. The mental wounds caused by Clint Longley's last-minute, game-winning pass last Thanksgiving were still fresh.

This game, it appeared, was over.

Kilmer, though, stood on the sidelines and vowed to script a happy ending.

"I got determined to take it down the field," he said.

He did. And it turned out the fun was just beginning. At least for the Redskins. Their fans soon witnessed one of the wildest, and weirdest, finishes in this rivalry's history:

A Kilmer-led touchdown; an overtime interception by "Captain Comeback" Roger Staubach; an unsportsmanlike conduct penalty on the usually cool Staubach and a Kilmer sneak for the winning score. The latter three rarely, if ever, occurred.

And it was a game in which Washington led only twice — 3-0 and 30-24, the final score. In between, the Redskins worked from behind. But Kilmer understood comebacks. He had crafted a career making them. In 1963, while playing for San Francisco, an auto accident nearly caused a foot to be amputated. He battled back, making a concession in his playing style, switching from a runner to a passer.

Four years later, New Orleans picked him in the expansion draft — highly-thought of quarterbacks aren't left unprotected. And when the Redskins traded for the 31-year-old Kilmer in 1971 — to be Sonny Jurgensen's backup — Kilmer's career was close to the end.

But that, too, was only beginning.

He led Washington in passing for six of the next seven years and guided the Redskins to victory over Dallas in the 1972 NFC Championship Game. Kilmer's career changed dramatically as he wrestled away the hearts of some fans who swore by his good buddy Jurgensen. Every time it seemed Kilmer was relegated to the bench, something would happen to Jurgensen and in came "Furnace Face." And good things happened.

"Billy didn't have the greatest ability, but he was a tough guy," said Washington linebacker Chris Hanburger. "He's the kind of guy you'd go into a fight with. He'd be the first one you'd pick."

In 1975 Kilmer was firmly in charge. Jurgensen had retired and coach George Allen didn't yet trust young Joe Theismann. Still, Kilmer had to prove he was capable as the Jurgensen safety net was yanked away.

"Everyone was going to be critical of me if I didn't throw well," said Kilmer, who would throw 23 touchdown passes that season, his Redskins high. "I probably trained harder than I did in previous seasons to improve my throwing and work on my fundamentals. I had never been formally a quarterback in college [at UCLA] and I had to work on my drops and setting myself.

"No doubt about it [the pressure increased]. I'd better show I can throw the ball better than I ever had. Sonny wasn't there to be a backup and everyone said I couldn't throw."

Resurrection was a Kilmer specialty. And a seven-point deficit was no trouble.

So with 5:03 remaining and the ball at Washington's 40-yard line, Kilmer, with more boos pounding his ears but not his confidence, spoke in the huddle: "Give me some protection and we'll take it down the field."

He got protection and the Redskins drove for the tie. A 24-yard pass to running back Mike Thomas moved the ball to the Dallas 21, followed by a 9-yard Thomas run on second down. Then, on fourth-and-2 from the 13, Thomas, after Kilmer called a time out, carried outside for six more. On the next play, Kilmer and tight end Jerry Smith hooked up for the touchdown with 1:52 left.

Kilmer later called this one of his most memo-

51

rable drives, fitting for a game that provided a steep pile of memories.

Dallas moved to the Washington 22 with 13 seconds remaining — thanks to four Staubach completions totalling 44 yards. But Toni Fritsch, who kicked a game-winner the previous week at Philadelphia, missed a 38-yard field-goal attempt to win the game.

Then came even more fun. At least for Washington.

The Cowboys won the toss and quickly penetrated Redskins' territory. Staubach connected with receiver Drew Pearson for 32 yards, giving Dallas a first down at the Washington 48 three plays into overtime.

On second-and-12 from midfield, Staubach dropped back to pass. Hanburger did not order a blitz. But, because he spotted the tight end lining up wide, Hanburger raced through the middle untouched. He arrived just as Staubach released the ball and his hit caused the pass to flutter downfield.

Safety Ken Houston intercepted the pass at the Washington 34 and returned it to the 50. Houston received a thigh contusion on the tackle and was probably done for the day. The damage was already done.

"Ken was a smart player," Staubach said, "and I probably shouldn't have thrown it. When he intercepted it, I just had a lump in my stomach."

But the real action occurred away from the ball. After Houston picked off the pass, Redskins cornerback Pat Fischer charged at Staubach.

"I must have run by their entire team to seek him out and block him," Fischer said. "I knocked him down and it was insignificant to the return, but I took advantage of the opportunity. I'd never gotten to hit him and he'd insulted me so many times [by completing passes]. I was delighted.

"He got up and was upset."

Just a little. Staubach had built a reputation as one of the league's classiest players. But he was also one of the most competitive. Not only was Staubach angered by the interception, he didn't like Fischer racing his way.

So, after the two bumped heads, Staubach elbowed Fischer, drawing a 15-yard penalty.

"He was coming to give me a dirty shot," Staubach recalled. "And I saw him coming and threw him to the ground, then jumped on him.

"He got up and laughed."

That penalty proved costly as Washington started its drive at the Dallas 35. After Kilmer gained three yards on first down, he went to the air.

A 9-yard pass to receiver Charley Taylor placed the ball at the 23. Then, on third-and-six from the 19, Kilmer again found Taylor, this time for eight yards.

Usually in such a situation, the Redskins would have run the ball, setting up the defensive-minded Allen's favorite score: the field goal. But kicker Mark Moseley had already missed from 29 and 45 yards.

"I got in the huddle and said, 'Look, we're going to score a touchdown because we're not going to let the field goal kicker miss another one,'" Kilmer recalled. "I was calling the plays. I know what George Allen wants me to run — he'll want me to run a dive play, something to get the ball in the middle of the field. I knew George would jump out of his shoes. I wish he were alive today to tell you what he thought. I know he died when I came out throwing."

Kilmer returned to the ground, however. Running backs Larry Brown and Mike Thomas combined for 10 yards to the 1. On first-and-goal, Kilmer tried something novel. He called for a sneak, his first of the season. It wasn't even in the playbook.

"I was in total shock that Billy Kilmer would sneak for a touchdown," said Dallas end Harvey Martin.

But he did. In the huddle, Kilmer told right guard Walt Sweeney, "I'm coming over you." Center Len Hauss helped Sweeney block left tackle Jethro Pugh to create the opening.

"[Middle linebacker] Lee Roy Jordan kept looking at me [before the snap] and I kept looking at him," Kilmer remembered. "At the last moment, he figured I was going to run a sneak. I took the ball and jumped, but when I jumped over, he hit me square in the jaw. He really got me."

Jordan didn't stop him, though. Nor could anyone prevent the fans from swarming onto the field after the game-winning score with 6:34 left in over-

Although this was the only occasion these teams met in overtime, each has played in numerous fifth quarters. Both have been successful in overtime, too: Washington is 10-9; Dallas 9-5.

time, ending one of the most exciting finishes in this rivalry. If it didn't top Longley's heroic heave the year before, it certainly came close.

While the fans cheered Kilmer in the end, they booed him much of the day. He finished with three touchdowns and 301 yards passing, his first 300-yard game since his second game with the Redskins in 1971. But he was picked off four times.

Kilmer admitted the last one, intercepted by Harris for the score, was a bad throw. Harris had fooled him into the toss. When Dallas blitzed, rather than stick tight on the receiver — in this case Brown — Harris laid off, hoping for an interception attempt.

"[Dallas coach Tom] Landry would get mad at me all the time for that," Harris said. "Sure enough, it worked this time. I read it and then started running at Billy. And I remember telling him, 'Billy, you don't want to tackle me.' "

Such big plays in this game weren't limited to the last few minutes of regulation and overtime. And the seven-point fourth-quarter lead wasn't Dallas' largest.

Washington contributed to its deficit with sloppy play. Kilmer's second interception, and the first of Harris' two pickoffs, led to a 10-yard Staubach to Pearson touchdown pass and a 14-3 lead.

Earlier, cornerback Mark Washington recovered a Thomas fumble, setting up another score as Staubach hit running back Preston Pearson from 12 yards out.

The Redskins recovered with Kilmer's 46-yard toss to receiver Frank Grant, making the score 14-10. But, following Fritsch's 33-yard field goal, Dallas positioned itself for a crushing blow with 32 seconds left in the first half.

The Cowboys were on the Redskins' 3 when Staubach attempted to pass. But Redskins end Ron McDole saved the day, and, perhaps the game. He bulled past tackle Rayfield Wright on the inside and slapped the ball out of Staubach's hands. McDole recovered and was tackled 15 yards later.

"I didn't realize just how big a play it was until after the game," McDole said. "When the game was going on, George just expected you to make plays like

that."

Much to Staubach's, and Dallas', chagrin.

"That could have put the game away," Staubach said.

Instead, it left the door ajar for Washington, which finally tied the score in the third on a leaping 2-yard catch by Taylor. That set up the fourth-quarter and overtime drama.

While the Redskins rallied on this day, the Cowboys had a knack for comebacks as well. Theirs started after this game, which left them in a three-way tie for first with 5-2 Washington and St. Louis. Dallas earned a wild-card berth with a 10-4 record, helped by a 31-10 thumping of Washington in the rematch.

Success followed in the playoffs. In the first round, Dallas beat Minnesota, 17-14, on Staubach's 50-yard Hail Mary touchdown pass to Drew Pearson. After crushing the Los Angeles Rams in the NFC Championship Game, Dallas lost to Pittsburgh, 21-17, in the Super Bowl.
Certainly the Cowboys' season wasn't ruined by the overtime loss at RFK.

And, with a young defensive line of Martin (third year), end Ed "Too Tall" Jones (second) and tackle Randy White (first), their future remained solid.

Meanwhile, the Redskins finished 8-6 and out of the playoffs. But they provided a lasting memory Nov. 2.

"For a bunch of old guys, over the hill," a hoarse Allen said after the game, "they looked pretty good in the fourth quarter. We beat those young whippersnappers."

REDSKINS 30, COWBOYS 24

	1	2	3	4	OT	TOTAL
COWBOYS	0	17	0	7	0	24
REDSKINS	3	7	7	7	6	30

◆ **FIRST QUARTER**
W - Moseley 43 FG, W 3-0

◆ **SECOND QUARTER**
D - P. Pearson 12 pass from Staubach (Fritsch kick), D 7-3
D - D. Pearson 10 pass from Staubach (Fritsch kick), D 14-3
W - Grant 46 pass from Kilmer (Moseley kick), D 14-10
D - Fritsch 33 FG, D 17-10

◆ **THIRD QUARTER**
W - Taylor 2 pass from Kilmer (Moseley kick), 17-17

◆ **FOURTH QUARTER**
D - Harris 27 interception return (Fritsch kick), D 24-17
W - Smith 7 pass from Kilmer (Moseley kick), 24-24

◆ **OVERTIME**
W - Kilmer 1 run, W 30-24

Diron Talbert

Diron Talbert hated Roger Staubach. That's why Talbert filed his own scouting report on the Dallas quarterback: 'Can't read defenses; afraid to get hit; easy to knock out.' Talbert, Washington's defensive tackle, always mouthed off during Dallas week, struggling to contain his dislike of Staubach.

It was a good act.

"Heavens yes, it was all in fun," said Talbert, a Redskin from 1971-80. "It was just game hype. If you go in treating the quarterback like Mary Poppins every week, it's hard to get yourself going. You don't have that many [personal] rivalries around. I don't know of any right now. You've got to have something to motivate you."

Ironically, Talbert considers Staubach a good friend these days. In 1984, Staubach and his family even stayed at Talbert's house during a visit to Washington. No one who followed either team would have guessed that would happen.

The Talbert-Staubach feud began after the 1972 NFC Championship Game, a 26-3 Washington victory. Staubach, who battled injuries that year, started in place of Craig Morton. After the nationally-televised game, sportscaster Jerry Kramer asked Talbert what the difference was. Talbert's response: "They started the wrong quarterback."

To which Staubach now says: "I still think that [statement] was a mistake. But that's the kind of thing that really made the rivalry so great."

It quickly escalated, with help from Redskins coach George Allen. Before playing Dallas, Allen and Talbert would discuss what each other would say. Their quotes filled the papers.

photo courtesy of the Washington Redskins

"George loved it," Talbert said. "He'd say, 'I'm going to say we'll get after them pretty good. And you can say, we're going to knock him out. There's nothing wrong with that. That should be your goal every play. But if you say 'I'll knock Staubach out,' everyone says, 'Oh, lord, watch out.' "

In 1975, a year after rookie Clint Longley's touchdown pass buried the Redskins, Talbert said, "Clint may be the best quarterback they've got."

That same season, he said of Staubach, "He's been in the league seven years and he still doesn't know how to read [defenses] very well."

The Redskins all laughed at this schtick. But they were convinced Staubach thought it was genuine. Once at a mid-1970s postseason banquet, Redskins Bill Brundige, Ron McDole and Talbert spotted Merlin Olsen and Staubach talking. So they walked over.

"Roger looked at Diron and said, absolutely sincere, 'Diron, why do you hate me so much? I don't hate you,' " Brundige recalled. "Diron just laughed."

Another time, Talbert and Staubach gathered at midfield with the other captains.

"I wouldn't shake hands with him, but I shook hands with everyone else," Talbert said. "Just to irritate him."

So what did Talbert really think of the Hall of Famer?

"I wish Staubach had been on our team," Talbert admitted. "He had so many different ways of scoring and pulling out big plays. He was the smartest quarterback."

Roger Staubach

He dodged defenders for an entire career — earning a nickname in the process — but one opponent proved tougher for Dallas quarterback Roger Staubach to shake. Staubach couldn't avoid the taunts and barbs slung by Washington defensive tackle Diron Talbert.

Nor could he counter them.

In the pregame coin toss one year, Talbert shook every Dallas captain's hands but Staubach's. So Staubach decided the next year, he'd reciprocate the snub.

"Diron told some reporters, 'Watch this, I'm going to go out there and I bet Staubach doesn't shake my hand,'" Staubach, a Hall of Famer, recalled. "Sure enough, he didn't initiate to shake my hand and everybody was watching. So then he kind of stuck his hand out and I didn't shake his hand like he did to me. But he had set it up. And then they wrote this article: 'Staubach is a poor sport, he wouldn't shake Talbert's hand before the game.'"

Their running rivalry — fed mostly by Talbert's pregame boasts of what would happen to Staubach if he scrambled — began in 1972 and lasted until Staubach's retirement in 1979. These days, they're friends and have played in numerous touch football games together.

When Staubach was inducted into the Washington Touchdown Club Hall of Fame, Talbert was one of his presenters.

But in their playing days . . .

"Diron used to give Roger a hell of a time," said Dallas running back Tony Dorsett, laughing at the memory. " 'Come on Captain America! Come on Roger!' [Talbert] was constantly badgering the guy. He couldn't rattle Roger. But sometimes it was funny and you couldn't help but laugh."

Staubach wasn't laughing after the 1972 NFC

photo courtesy of the Dallas Cowboys

Championship Game. Not only were the Cowboys drubbed, 26-3, Staubach was awful. Afterward, Talbert told reporters that Dallas coach Tom Landry started the wrong guy.

That rankled the competitive Staubach, who said that statement was "bush" and "tasteless." Later, he admitted he didn't play well, but Staubach still got riled. Before a Thanksgiving Day game in 1974, Talbert predicted a Staubach knockout, which wound up happening.

"Next time, they'll have to kill me," Staubach said.

"It was just Roger's intensity," said Dallas center John Fitzgerald. "It just galled him. And I'd drive him to the charter [on road games]. And when it was Washington, it was like, 'Roger, calm down, we have a little time to go before we play. Please, let me rest. We have a day to go yet.'"

Still, Staubach never lost his cool. Except once. After throwing an overtime interception in a 1975 loss, Staubach took a swipe at cornerback Pat Fischer, drawing a 15-yard penalty. Ten plays and 35 yards later, quarterback Billy Kilmer scored on a sneak.

Naturally, Washington coach George Allen attributed the penalty to the Redskins' weeklong digs at Staubach.

But whenever Dallas defeated Washington, Staubach refused to gloat. He could have as he held the upper hand. Against the Redskins, Staubach finished 9-7 as a starter and completed 50.1 percent of his passes, compared to 57 percent for his career, with 16 touchdowns and 15 interceptions.

Another number matters more.

"It seems like he's got a lot more Super Bowl rings than we did," Talbert said.

Staubach had finally upstaged Talbert, 2-0.

photo by The Associated Press

Dallas' Harvey Martin has a special delivery for a somber Redskins locker room in 1979.

Dec. 16, 1979

Roger Dodges Defeat
Cowboys 35, Redskins 34

Roger Staubach deliberately broke from the huddle, settling into shotgun formation behind center John Fitzgerald, whose hands rested on the ball at the 8-yard line. Fullback Ron Springs was to Staubach's immediate right, running back Preston Pearson to the Dallas quarterback's left, backfield body guards just inside the 15.

The Texas Stadium crowd, 62,867 strong on this cool Sunday evening, was on its feet, noisily anticipating what it could never have dreamed, not this moment – 42 seconds left in the final game of the 1979 season, and the two-time defending NFC champion Dallas Cowboys facing second-and-goal trailing 34-28.

Those despised Washington Redskins were on the other side of the ball. That darn Diron Talbert. And Dave Butz. And Coy Bacon. And that hard-nosed guy from Christoval, Texas, Jack Pardee, a disciple of hated former Washington coach George Allen, was over there on the sideline, coaching these Redskins.

The NFC East Division title hung in balance. The Cowboys were 10-5. The Redskins were 10-5. Philadelphia was 10-5. The winner of this 60-minute tug-of-war would be division champs. The loser might get a wild-card berth into the playoffs. Might.

Millions across the nation listened to those hallowed tones of CBS TV broadcaster Pat Summerall, painting the spine-chilling drama in his unique economy of words. Radios brought to life the words of Cowboys play-by-play man Brad Sham, who was doing his best to keep Charlie Waters, Cowboys injured safety turned color analyst for the day, from jumping out of the booth. Waters had proclaimed this entire game, despite the Cowboys having trailed by as many as 17 points in the first half and by 13 with eight minutes remaining, "You gotta believe."

Right Charlie.

"It was like a Super Bowl in Texas Stadium," Cowboys wide receiver Tony Hill said. "They were pumped. I had never heard a crowd so loud at Texas Stadium."

But right there, in the middle of this emotional hurricane, with every second and every step stuffed with far-reaching ramifications, Staubach just froze time – momentarily halting this fast-forwarded action as he stared down at the Redskins, remembering what their defense had done in a similar situa-

tion the last time Dallas coach Tom Landry had called the play he was planning to run.

"Up in Washington, the same predicament," Staubach said. "I just remembered in Washington."

Sure Staubach remembered "up in Washington" that season. All the Cowboys did. It was only four weeks ago. The memory of that 34-20 loss to Washington was fresh in their minds, having been sandwiched in the middle of a three-game losing streak for the NFC team that had played in the past two Super Bowls. And these Cowboys were seething, still, remembering most how Washington, leading, 31-20, with 14 seconds left and the Cowboys out of timeouts – out of Staubach miracles – called a timeout so Mark Moseley could kick a 45-yard field goal.

The nerve, these Cowboys cried. This overt pouring of salt in the wound had moved their emotional defensive end Harvey Martin to scream, "The next time we play them, we'll chop their heads off."

Some 18 years later, Martin said, "We were all pissed off. But you've got to understand, with the Cowboys and the Redskins playing each other, and the Redskins get up on you, why not kick a field goal? I'd do the same thing to them. Same thing. Get them down, and keep beating them."

For their part, the Redskins say they were concerned about point differential in the event of a tie, remembering 1973 when the first-place tie between the Cowboys and Redskins for the NFC East title was broken on the basis of Dallas outscoring Washington by 13 points in their two-game series. Problem now was, points were the fifth tie-breaking consideration.

But if this had inspired the Cowboys, it sure took a while on this cloudy day. The Redskins had jumped to a 17-0 lead just two minutes into the second quarter. The Cowboys already had fumbled the opening kickoff, fumbled the ball away on the second play from scrimmage and again on their next possession.

And evidently that funeral-styled wreath sent from a florist in Rockville, Md., directly to the Cowboys' practice facility wishing "sympathy" for the impending loss had little effect, too. And surprisingly so, since Martin, incensed by the dark gesture, stewed all week long, setting up the flowers in front of his locker for incentive.

'I got to thinking, 'Man, that means I'm dead or something. They sent me a wreath,' " Martin said. "I just kept looking at it. So on the way to the stadium, I told Buck [equipment manager Buchanan], 'Buck, bring that wreath with us. Take that thing to Texas Stadium.' "

Springs had scored on a 1-yard run in the second quarter, but nothing really seemed to jump start the Cowboys until 34-year-old Preston Pearson took matters into his experienced, third-down hands. The Cowboys had been decimated by injuries. Running back Tony Dorsett was out. Waters was out. Safety Randy Hughes was out. So was defensive tackle Jethro Pugh. Defensive end Ed "Too Tall" Jones was off boxing. And linebacker Thomas "Hollywood" Henderson had been "cut" just after the first Washington game.

But trailing 17-7, with just 1:48 left in the half, Staubach moved the Cowboys from their own 15, to the Redskins' 16 with 29 seconds to spare. Hill caught three passes for 46 yards. Pearson had one for 20. And a holding call moved the Cowboys back to the Washington 26, third-and-20 with just 15 seconds left. Enter Pearson.

"The weak safety bit on the inside move, which we knew he would do," Pearson said. "I was able to get behind him and Roger put the ball up there. He put it near the back of the end zone, and I didn't think I had a chance, and wasn't sure if I could keep my feet in the end zone."

Pearson did all of that, shaving the lead to 17-14 and giving the Cowboys a breath of life.

Certainly Staubach, preparing to bark out those last minute goal-line signals, remembered taking a 21-17 lead on fullback Robert Newhouse's 1-yard run early in the third quarter. Undoubtedly he recalled the 17 consecutive points the Redskins had score, at the time leaving Joe Theismann, John Riggins and the rest of those Redskins sitting mighty pretty, leading 34-21, in this winner-take-all duel with just 6:54 to play.

And for sure, if not Staubach, then Cowboys strong safety Dennis Thurman remembered what appeared to have been the conclusive touchdown, Riggins, the toughest Redskin of all, quaking by him for a 66-yard touchdown to create the 13-point margin.

"The first game I ever started," said Thurman, an 11th-round draft choice in 1978. "I remember Riggins hitting the sideline and turning up on the play. I took a poor angle and he was obviously faster than I thought. I ended up diving at him trying to catch him."

Game, set, division title – so it seemed.

"They were beating the hell out of us," then Cowboys president Tex Schramm said.

But for sure, Staubach also remembered bringing his team back three other times in the final two minutes that season. He wasn't giving up, especially not after narrowing the lead to 34-28 when defensive tackle Randy White's recovery of running back Clarence Harmon's fumble set up his 26-yard touchdown pass to Springs. And certainly not defensive tackle Larry Cole gave them one last chance.

"To write the script, you have to have all the pieces," Cole said.

Here's his piece: The two-minute warning had sounded. The Redskins still led 34-28. They faced a third-and-2. Riggins already had gained 153 yards and scored two touchdowns. One more first down and the title was Washington's.

"It was kind of entertaining," Waters remembered of the broadcast many in the parking lots were now listening to, "because Brad had been pooh-poohing it, saying, 'It's over' early, and then all of a sudden Brad says, 'Shame on all you Cowboys fans for [leaving].' I remember saying earlier, 'You gotta believe,' because Brad was kind of hard, saying, 'Ah Charlie what do you mean? You don't have a chance.' And I'm saying, 'No, no ...' Hey I was a homer, I know."

But Waters wound up being an accurate homer.

"They had run this play earlier where the center [Ted Fritsch] cuts off the tackle and they do a toss to the outside," Cole said. "It usually worked because they had a darn good center.' "

At the snap – the crowd chanting, "Defense, defense ..." – Cole gambled, knifing at a sharp angle to his left with no regard for reading keys. Center Fritsch couldn't get to him fast enough, rolling harmlessly to the ground on his back.

"Riggins was tooling around the corner, and I'm sure he was surprised I was there," Cole said. "And when I hit him, and tackled him, it was like the whole crowd was making the tackle. It was electrifying.' "

Not for the Redskins, the 2-yard loss forcing them to punt. The Cowboys had the ball back, and they knew Staubach had fashioned 10 previous come-from-behind fourth-quarter rallies in his career, six in the final two minutes. And he had another chance, first-and-10 at his 25, with 1:46 to go.

"We were behind, but you could look into their defensive guys eyes, and it was like, 'Ah, hell, we gave them too much time,' " Fitzgerald said. "They knew we were going to score. Dead knew it."

The Redskins received a better clue on the first play when Hill beat cornerback Joe Lavender for a 20-yard gain. Two plays later, Staubach somehow ducked under defensive tackle Perry Brooks' rush, and teamed up with Pearson, who beat rookie linebacker Monte Coleman for 22 yards. A play later,

Staubach again goes to Pearson, who beats Coleman for 25 yards.

"He wasn't ready for me," Pearson said of the 11th-round pick. "I had too much stuff."

Unbelievable, there the Cowboys were, at the Redskins' 8, and still 45 seconds remained. An incompletion to Hill took three seconds. In came the play from Landry, "Hot Left 17," basically a quick pass to tight end Billy Joe DuPree.

Yet, in all this commotion, with so much having transpired and so much on the line, Staubach coolly recalled, "We called that play in Washington, and they blitzed everybody, and I got trapped. So I told Tony, 'Hey if they blitz make a good move on [cornerback Lemar] Parrish.'"

Hill has his own version, recalling walking into the huddle and saying, "Hey Rog, I can beat him on a nine [route].' And he says, 'If I look your way, I'm coming your way.' See if they come up and bump-and-run on us we do the fade.

"So we go to the line and he looks at me."

Staubach then checked to see if the Redskins were coming. Yes, they were. Every one of them. So he glanced knowingly at Hill to his right, eye contact their only communication. Fitzgerald snapped the ball.

Pearson and Springs did their jobs, keeping the pocket free of Redskins. Hill faked in, froze Parrish and then faded out slightly to his right. Staubach took one step back, and off his back foot lofted the ball for Hill, who made an easy over-the-shoulder catch running into the end zone. Touchdown – 35-34 Cowboys.

"You know you have a shot, and your instincts take over," Staubach said of what turned out to be his final, last-minute comeback recurring concussions convincing him to retire before the 1980 season.

"I was pumped, pumped up," Hill said. "You would have thought I was on some kind of drugs."

The Redskins? Well, things were bad. St. Louis had lost to Chicago that day 42-6, meaning they would be eliminated from the playoffs. Coleman and Fritsch openly wept on the field. Defensive end Dallas Hickman, so frustrated, cracked his helmet slamming it into the ground.

And as if all this were not bad enough for Washington, steamed over losing, steamed over being denied a timeout with one second left and the chance at a game-winning 58-yard field goal try, Martin de-cided to add to the Redskins' misery.

"We're jumping up and down in the locker room," Martin said, "and this guy, [rookie cornerback] Wade Manning, came to me and says, 'Harvey, Harvey what are you going to do with the wreath?' I just snapped. I grabbed the wreath, walked out the door, asked directions to the visiting team's locker room – I had never been there – I walked up, opened the door, threw the wreath into the middle of their prayer and told them, 'Take this damn thing back to Washington with you.'"

The wreath skidded into the leg of Moseley, the one he didn't get to use in that final second.

"Harvey was just Harvey," Talbert said. "He had something rubbed in his face earlier, and he was just getting back. I would have done the same thing if I had thought about it."

Harvey thought about it later, though, as Landry chastised him the next day after front-page pictures captured Martin, in full uniform – helmet and all – carrying the wreath toward the Redskins locker room. He would send telegrams of apology to the Redskins and both Washington newspapers. And to this day, even though Washington Star reporter Betty Cuniberti traced the wreath's sender down to a Cowboys fan in Rockville – he was trying to psyche up his team – Martin isn't buying.

"Yeah, I still believe [the Redskins] sent it to me," Martin says. "See after the game, here comes the backlash: 'It was actually sent by a Cowboys fan to get you fired up, Harvey.' That's bull. That came from Washington. A Cowboys fan? No sir, I don't believe that. Hey, they didn't like me, I didn't like them."

Just that simple. Cowboys and Indians forever, and not even time can thaw these frozen memories.

COWBOYS 35, REDSKINS 34

	1	2	3	4	TOTAL
COWBOYS	0	14	7	14	35
REDSKINS	10	7	0	17	34

◆ **FIRST QUARTER**
W - Moseley 24 FG, W 3-0
W - Theismann 1 run (Moseley kick), W 10-0

◆ **SECOND QUARTER**
W - Malone 55 pass from Theismann (Moseley kick), W 17-0
D - Springs 1 run (Septien kick), W 17-7
D - P. Pearson 26 pass from Staubach (Septien kick), W 17-14

◆ **THIRD QUARTER**
D - Newhouse 2 run (Septien kick), D 21-17

◆ **FOURTH QUARTER**
W - Moseley 24 FG, D 21-20
W - Riggins 1 run (Moseley kick), W 27-21
W - Riggins 66 run (Moseley kick), W 34-21
D - Springs 26 pass from Staubach (Septien kick), W 34-28
D - Hill 7 pass from Staubach (Septien kick), D 35-34

photo by Arnie Sachs/Consolidated News Pictures

Washington defensive tackle Dexter Manley knocks out Dallas quarterback Danny White in the 1982 NFC Championship Game.

Jan. 22, 1983

We Want Dallas

Redskins 31, Cowboys 17

The Dallas Cowboys traveled to Washington for the 1982 NFC Championship Game with their bags supposedly packed for the Super Bowl.

Why not? The Cowboys had beaten the Redskins six straight times and had won three in a row at RFK Stadium, including a convincing 24-10 triumph just seven weeks earlier. Naturally, the Cowboys playing in their third straight NFC title game and their fifth in six years, expected to win.

"We thought we'd be the ones in the Super Bowl," Dallas receiver Drew Pearson said despite the locker room dissension about the players' strike which had wiped out seven weeks of the season.

And the Super Bowl was in just eight days. The strike had cancelled the normal two-week break between the conference championship games and the Super Bowl. The winner at RFK was due in Pasadena, Calif., the next night to begin preparations for Super Bowl XXVII so the Cowboys' rumored travel plans were logical.

However, when the news reached Redskin Park, a fire was lit.

"When we heard that Dallas was packed to go straight from RFK to Pasadena, that was all we needed," said Redskins defensive tackle Darryl Grant. "It was the ultimate insult. They had been to the Super Bowl [but not since 1978]. They had all the high-profile players. They were going to come into our backyard and dance all over us, business as usual, and go on to Pasadena. The coaches had to pull us off each other a little bit in practice after we found out because we were so intense. Guys were playing the game on Friday."

That fuse was still burning as kickoff approached on Saturday.

"I can't remember ever seeing guys so ready to go," Grant said. "We were focused and committed. Guys were angrily taping their wrists. There was a lot of talk about 'no respect.' We could hardly wait to get on the field. We were hyperventilating."

So were the Washington fans, who hadn't played host to a championship game in a decade. The chant of "We Want Dallas" which had reverberated around the stadium during the playoff victories over Detroit and Minnesota, reached fever pitch as the player introductions and kickoff approached.

"We were sitting in the locker room and you could just hear that stadium bouncing and the fans screaming, 'We Want Dallas,' " said Redskins guard Russ Grimm. "It sent a chill down your spine."

Mark Moseley, who that year became the only kicker in NFL history to be named the league's Most Valuable Player, said "I don't think Dallas ever had a chance."

The Cowboys, used to the quiet confines of Texas Stadium, were intimidated.

"The crowd was unbelievable," said Cowboys star halfback Tony Dorsett. "You talk about feeling like someone's sticking a dagger in your back. You could tell they were waiting for us and had wanted us for a while. That place was rocking."

But so was the Dallas offense early. Quarterback Danny White led the Cowboys 75 yards on their opening drive, hitting Pearson for a key 24-yard gain, before the march finally stalled at the Washington 10. Rafael Septien's 27-yard field goal made it 3-0 for the visitors. It would prove to be their only lead.

The Redskins stormed right back, moving 84 yards in nine plays, the last a 19-yard pass from quarterback Joe Theismann to receiver Charlie Brown – running a post pattern – for the go-ahead touchdown with 1:55 left in the first quarter.

Washington failed to increase its lead on its next possession only because Moseley – who had gone strangely cold in the playoffs after hitting 21-of-22 field goal attempts during the season – missed from 27 yards. But six minutes later, all Moseley had to do was tack on the extra point. Tony Peters had stripped the Cowboys' Rod Hill on a punt return and Washington's Monte Coleman had recovered at the Dallas 11. Four plays later, running back John Riggins bulled over from the 1, giving the Redskins a 14-3 lead.

With 32 seconds to go before halftime, Washington defensive end Dexter Manley crumpled White. The quarterback walked off the field, but the concussion ended his season. After the game, White was still so disoriented that he couldn't remember the play. In White's absence, the Cowboys turned to Gary Hogeboom, a third-year pro from Central Michigan who had thrown just eight career passes.

"We didn't feel that it was over," Dorsett said of the seemingly hopeless situation. "Anytime you lose your starter, you've got to expect a little dropoff, but we thought we had capable people to come in and get the job done. We rallied around that guy."

That's exactly what happened. After Nick Giaquinto saved Washington by recovering Mike Nelms' fumble of the second-half kickoff, the Redskins went nowhere. Jeff Hayes' shanked punt gave Dallas the ball on the Washington 38. It took Hogeboom just six plays to produce a touchdown as he hit Pearson for the 6-yard score.

Nelms redeemed himself by returning the subsequent kickoff 76 yards on what Redskins coach Joe Gibbs said was "maybe the key play of the game." Theismann then found Brown for 22 yards to set up Riggins' 4-yard touchdown.

Unruffled by the 11-point deficit, Hogeboom again moved the Cowboys. Dorsett finally broke loose on a 17-yard run and Hogeboom finished off the 14-play, 84-yard drive with a 23-yard strike to receiver Butch Johnson. The Redskins had been relaxed enough with the big lead to concern themselves with yanking off the little towels worn by the Cowboys' skill position players. Now they watched helplessly as Johnson dropped to his knees and fired imaginary six-shooters in the end zone in celebration. Dallas had closed within 21-17 with 3:25 still left in the *third* quarter.

"We were getting real nervous," said Washington linebacker Mel Kaufman.

With good reason. Hogeboom's pass to tight end Doug Cosbie on the first play of the fourth quarter put the Cowboys on the Washington 25.

Dorsett gained five, but Peters then came up from his strong safety spot and dumped Dorsett for a 3-yard loss. When Hogeboom couldn't connect with reserve running back Timmy Newsome on third down, Septien came on. His 42-yard field goal try missed wide right.

However, Dallas got the ball right back after defensive end Ed "Too Tall" Jones tackled Riggins shy of a first down on third-and-1. The Cowboys took over at their 32, but Redskins defensive coordinator Richie Petitbon – who had missed out on playing in Washington's 1972 NFC Championship Game victory over Dallas because of a knee injury – and his well-coached players were about to take over.

Kaufman and Jeris White had come up with a scheme where the cornerback would line up inside of the linebacker when they expected a particular Dallas pass play. They went into their trick mode on first down and Hogeboom, seeing White moving inside, threw an out to receiver Tony Hill. Kaufman, dropping back into coverage, made the leaping interception, his first of the year. That pickoff and Theismann's 26-yard completion to Brown set up Moseley's 29-yard field goal.

With 7:12 still to play and trailing just 24-17, the Cowboys still had hope. But not for long. Petitbon and Co. figured Hogeboom's first-down call from his 20 would be a screen for Dorsett that had earlier picked up 25 yards. They figured right.

"I tried to get in the middle of the screen to disrupt it," Grant said. "The ball was tipped [by Manley]. I looked up and saw it. I just ran underneath it with my hands stuck out. It seemed like it took forever to come down, like it was in slow motion. I was just saying in my mind, 'Catch it and go. Catch it and go.'"

That's what Grant did as he high-stepped into the end zone with the interception for the touch-

From 1970-83, the Redskins and Cowboys combined for 11 trips to the NFC Championship Game, twice playing each other. Overall, Washington is 5-0 at home in the NFC title game, beating Dallas in 1972 and 1982, San Francisco in 1983, Minnesota in 1987 and Detroit in 1991. But the Redskins lost at the New York Giants in 1986. Dallas is 8-6 in championship games, but just 4-5 on the road.

down, turned to the Dallas bench, and spiked the ball before being mobbed by his teammates.

"I couldn't believe it happened," Hogeboom lamented. "It was a simple screen."

Down 31-17 with the Washington fans roaring, Hogeboom refused to quit. He hit Pearson for 16 on the next play and Johnson for 13 on third-and-5 to give Dallas a first down on the Washington 38. But Hogeboom's next four passes fell incomplete, ending the Cowboys' Pasadena plans.

Hogeboom completed 14-of-29 passes for 162 yards (12 more than Theismann) and the Cowboys outgained the Redskins, 340-260. But the opportunistic Washington defense and the running game of Riggins and the young offensive line known as the Hogs made the difference.

Riggins, the runner nicknamed "The Diesel" because of his power, carried on the next nine plays after the Redskins got the ball back to virtually run out the clock and push his totals to 140 yards on 36 carries for the day and a staggering 444 yards on 98 carries in Washington's trio of playoff victories.

"On the third or fourth 50-Gut [Riggins up the middle], I told Russ, 'Let's have some fun,' " said Redskins center Jeff Bostic. "We're the young kids on the block. We're the nobodies. The Cowboys walked the field as if their feet didn't touch the ground. They were 'America's Team' and all that. We came to the line and told [Dallas veteran Pro Bowl defensive tackle] Randy White, 'We're running the ball at you.' He didn't say anything."

Maybe White and the aging Cowboys, who had been to the playoffs 15 times in 16 years, sensed that their day was finally ending. They wouldn't win another postseason game for nine years.

"We'll probably be labeled as the team that can't win the big ones," Dorsett said after the Cowboys' third straight NFC title loss.

Pearson acknowledged that the better team had triumphed.

"It's their year," Pearson said. "They made the plays to make it happen. It's the year of the Redskin."

More like the decade.

In the 11 seasons starting in 1982, Washington won three Super Bowls, four NFC titles and 16 playoff games.

"That's when the tide turned a little bit," Grimm said of the first triumph in a stretch where Washington took four of five from Dallas.

But that day all that mattered to the Redskins and their frenzied fans was that they had finally beaten the hated Cowboys. Not even the upcoming Super Bowl was as important.

"We were so excited about beating Dallas that it took about 20 minutes before it sunk in that we were going to the Super Bowl," said Grant, one of 38 players who had never before beaten the Cowboys as a Redskin.

"This was the way it was supposed to be," Gibbs said in the wild locker room after having been carried off the field and then accepting a congratulatory phone call from President Ronald Reagan. "I haven't even thought about the Super Bowl. This is our Super Bowl. This was everything rolled into one. The Redskins versus Dallas, the team we wanted to beat the most. How can you top that?"

The Redskins seemingly did in the Super Bowl, rallying from a 17-10 halftime deficit to beat the AFC Champion Miami Dolphins, 27-17, thanks to Riggins' 166 yards, including the game-winning 43-yard touchdown run on 4th-and-inches.

But to those who were at RFK on that January afternoon, nothing could be sweeter than trouncing the Cowboys just to get to the big game.

"I never heard RFK so loud," Grant said.

Or so happy.

REDSKINS 31, COWBOYS 17

	1	2	3	4	TOTAL
COWBOYS	3	0	14	0	17
REDSKINS	7	7	7	10	31

◆ FIRST QUARTER
D - Septien 27 FG, D 3-0
W - Brown 19 pass from Theismann (Moseley kick), W 7-3

◆ SECOND QUARTER
W - Riggins 1 run (Moseley kick), W 14-3

◆ THIRD QUARTER
D - Pearson 6 pass from Hogeboom (Septien kick), W 14-10
W - Riggins 4 run (Moseley kick), W 21-10
D - Johnson 23 pass from Hogeboom (Septien kick), W 21-17

◆ FOURTH QUARTER
W - Moseley 29 FG, W 24-17
W - Grant 10 interception return (Moseley kick), W 31-17

photo by The Washington Times

Dallas running back Timmy Newsome picks up yardage in a come-from-behind victory in the 1983 opener.

Sept. 5, 1983

White Lightning

Cowboys 31, Redskins 30

He had left the RFK Stadium field only eight months earlier, escorted through a swarm of fans, his mind blanketed in a mental fog. Dallas quarterback Danny White had been pounded, roughed up and knocked out by Washington's defense.

After Redskins defensive end Dexter Manley dumped him on the painted turf, White wobbled to the sideline, a concussion victim. Later, after Washington captured the NFC championship, White was hounded en route to the locker room by a drunken Redskins fan, who mouthed off to him.

So White grabbed him with his right hand and conked him with his left before police intervened.

These poundings escaped White's memory. But the offseason beating in the press didn't. White became an easy target as Dallas once again realized that he was no Roger Staubach.

For three years, White tried to wrench himself free of Staubach's daunting shadow. It followed White constantly and each time he failed to guide the Cowboys to the Super Bowl, the shadow swallowed him whole. No matter that White would end up throwing the most touchdown passes in Dallas history (155), he had two flaws: His first name wasn't Roger; and he never appeared in a Super Bowl. The Cowboys were 0-3 in NFC title games since Staubach's retirement in 1979.

"Everybody wanted to see us win the big one and everyone wanted to know if Danny was the answer," said Dallas running back Tony Dorsett, who played with both quarterbacks. "Some of it was unfair, but when you're playing for 'America's Team,' people expect big things of you. But Danny handled it well and proved himself deserving of the position."

Also, some Cowboys criticized White for his role in the 1982 strike. At one point, after meeting with Dallas president Tex Schramm, White tried to convince his teammates that management's offer, with the wording changed in a few places, was acceptable.

This divided the Cowboys as player representative Robert Newhouse disagreed. White, who said he was just trying to help settle the strike, got labeled as pro-management.

"I was pro-settlement," White said.

Still, "It touched a lot of people, touched them deeply," Dorsett said. "It cut deep with certain individuals, I'm sure even to this day. People haven't forgotten some of the things that took place at that time."

Those problems escalated following the 1982 NFC Championship Game loss to Washington. When Dallas reported to camp the next summer, White found himself needing to beat out Gary Hogeboom, who had replaced him in that title game, as the starter.

"A lot of people gravitated toward Gary because of the position Danny took during the strike," said Dallas receiver Drew Pearson, who was Staubach's go-to guy, but not White's. "[Coach Tom] Landry declared Danny the starter and you had to suck it up and play with him. But in the locker room, Danny wasn't very popular."

White, booed in the preseason, said, "Through it all, I had to guard my personal life and my private feelings. I just kept telling myself that all of these things are part of being the starting quarterback."

So he had dealt with a difficult offseason. Surprisingly, so, too had the Redskins.

The defending Super Bowl champions had to address a USFL defection (guard Fred Dean), a holdout (cornerback Jeris White), a grievance filed over 1982 contract incentives (kicker Mark Moseley) and an indictment for conspiring to sell cocaine (safety Tony Peters).

Next came a 2-2 preseason, including a 38-7 stomping by Miami.

"Everyone said, 'Hey, those guys are getting fat and happy,'" said Washington guard Mark May. "We had a terrible preseason."

Still, as the season rolled around — and the hype for this Monday Night game reached championship game level — Washington remained confident. And the Redskins embarked on a quest to prove their title wasn't tainted by the 57-day strike. Their first victims, everyone figured, would be the Cowboys, whom Manley referred to as "punks" the week of the game.

One of the biggest questions plaguing the Hogs before this game was: Limo or no limo? A local limousine service offered to drive them to RFK Stadium. The Hogs, Washington's famous offensive line, declined. Maybe after the game, they said.

That wouldn't be necessary. After this game, no Redskins felt like celebrating.

But that would have been tough to foresee at halftime as everything had clicked for Washington. Moseley booted a 23-yard field goal and fullback John Riggins scored on a 1-yard run for a 10-0 first-quarter lead.

Even when things looked bad, they wound up positive for the Redskins.

On second-and-10 from the Dallas 17, Dorsett burst free. He sped down the left sideline, flying by the Redskins' bench, and everyone understood how these scenes ended — Dorsett scored. No one caught him.

Almost no one.

Before Washington's rookie cornerback Darrell Green had been drafted in the first round, some friends asked him if he thought he'd be able to chase down Dorsett. Green didn't know.

But Green, who started this game as Jeris White continued to hold out, soon got his answer. When Dorsett began his jaunt, Green bolted from the other side of the field and showed his world-class speed. He pulled down Dorsett at the 6-yard line.

"My brain didn't register, 'This is Tony Dorsett,'" Green said. "I remember running past our whole defense. Shoo! Shoo! Shoo! Like cars going by. I had to run a long way and didn't just run across the field, I caught him from behind."

Dorsett, of course, was shocked.

"For most of that run, another guy was chasing me and I could see him out of the corner of my eye," Dorsett recalled. "But I had my vision blocked from Darrell. All of a sudden, Darrell pulls up beside me and I'm like, 'Dang, where did he come from?' If I had seen him from the beginning, I wouldn't have let him catch me. It was a great effort on his part."

One guy wasn't surprised: Redskins coach Joe Gibbs.

"One of the most amazing things I saw in sports was Darrell running the 40-yard dash," Gibbs said.

That speed, which has stayed around 4.2 seconds in the 40 throughout Green's long career, is what intrigued the Redskins when he played at Division II Texas A&I. But Green later fretted that his chasing down of Dorsett would label him as "just a speed guy."

What it really did is cost Dallas four points as the Cowboys settled for a 26-yard Rafael Septien field goal.

Washington continued to pound away. The Redskins added two more field goals for a 16-3 lead.

First Moseley ended a 13-play drive with a 30-yarder and then his 39-yarder punctuated a six-play series.

But even more Redskins points would follow. Another forced punt — Dallas' fourth of the half — and a 22-yard Mike Nelms return gave Washington the ball on its own 43. With 40 seconds remaining in the half and facing second-and-16, quarterback Joe Theismann connected with receiver Charlie Brown for a 41-yard score.

At halftime, the Redskins led, 23-3. They had controlled the ball for 22:35, piled up 261 total yards to the Cowboys' 85 — 77 of which came on Dorsett's run — and had 12 more first downs than the visitors. Theismann had thrown for 181 yards — 80 of which went to receiver Alvin Garrett, whom announcer Howard Cosell referred to as "that little monkey" during the broadcast; Riggins had rushed for 64. Televisions across the country clicked off.

"We were rolling it up," May said. "We thought the game was over and we were unstoppable."

But, ironically, the domination took its toll on this hot, humid night.

"The first half had to be the longest half ever played in football," said Redskins offensive tackle Joe Jacoby. "I came in [to the locker room] and had to change everything because of how drenched I was. We spent ourselves."

Something else occurred in the Dallas locker room. Danny White vented his frustration stemming from a poor first half. He had completed just 1-of-9 passes for 10 yards and his critics had to be howling.

This on the heels of his lackluster championship game performance.

"It was an embarrassment," White said after the game. "I can't think of a worse first half we have played offensively.

"I was burning up. I was throwing helmets; fumes were coming out of my ears. "

But Dallas coach Tom Landry said he never considered yanking White, who didn't think he deserved such a fate anyway. Nor did he want to leave. Despite getting bopped around all half, White said, "I wasn't going to let myself get knocked out again."

Instead, White and Landry huddled with receiver Tony Hill to discuss strategy. Hill, the Cowboys' leading wideout the past four seasons, noticed that the Redskins' secondary faked double coverage against him at the line of scrimmage. But one of the defenders would drop off. That left room for Hill to get open down the sideline.

Two minutes into the third quarter, this skull session paid dividends. Hill ran a fly pattern, toasting cornerback Vernon Dean for a 75-yard touchdown catch. Dean had not heard a defensive audible and expected help over the middle from safety Mark Murphy. He didn't get it. In 1982, the secondary was a strong point, but with the holdout and drug problems, it would become known as the "Pearl Harbor Crew" for its weekly bombings.

Suddenly, the Cowboys had a spark and it continued to grow. Washington tried to answer, reaching the Dallas 26. But a 10-yard holding penalty on tight end Clint Didier and 10-yard sack of Theismann took the Redskins out of field goal range. Jeff Hayes' 27-yard punt gave the Cowboys a first down on their 19.

White returned to work. On third-and-10 from the 49, Hill raced down the right sideline with nickel back Anthony Washington trailing closely. Hill caught White's toss at the 20, Washington fell, and the 51-yard touchdown pass cut the deficit to 23-17.

There was still 7:35 remaining in the third quarter. Suddenly, RFK Stadium's 55,045 fans had lost their bounce. Dallas had gained its stride.

"It just clicked," Dorsett said. "If you've ever been involved in a big rivalry, pride comes into play. When you've got pride, you don't just sit around and let them totally manhandle you. We knew we had to come back out and show what we were made of."

Again Washington threatened. Again miscues cost the Redskins. Tight end Don Warren caught an 8-yard pass on third-and-5 from the Dallas 13. But Warren was flagged for interference, pushing the ball to the 24. One play later, Moseley — a career 82 percent kicker inside the 40 to this point — missed a 31-yard field goal try with 9:24 left in the game.

The Cowboys accepted the gift. White and Dorsett led an 80-yard go-ahead touchdown march that gobbled up 6:59 and ended when White scored on a 1-yard bootleg. On the drive, White completed two passes for 25 yards and Dorsett carried three times for 27 yards. A 15-yard personal foul on Redskins linebacker Mel Kaufman was a big help to Dallas, now leading 24-23.

The collapse continued when, two plays after White's score, Theismann, who finished with 325 yards passing, was intercepted by defensive back Ron Fellows. He returned the pass 33 yards to the Washington 4. Three plays later, White hit tight end Doug Cosbie for a 1-yard score. With 1:49 remaining, the Cowboys led, 31-23. A game that

once seemed over for Dallas was now finished for Washington.

The Redskins added a late touchdown, but only eight seconds remained, and Dallas won.

"Part of you is humiliated, but the other part of you looks back and thinks, 'They're pretty good,' " Walker said. "To spot you 20 points and come back and beat you at your place — on Monday Night — adds a flair to it."

May said, "That was a great lesson to learn as young players that we're not any better than we think we are. That [loss] was the best thing that happened to us."

It looked that way as Washington won 14 of its next 15 games. But Dallas used this game as a springboard as well, winning its first seven games, thanks to White. The straight-laced White shouted and celebrated in the locker room, reveling in these second-half passing numbers: 8-of-10 for 183 yards and three touchdowns. White won a game the Staubach way with a dazzling comeback.

"He showed everyone on national television what we knew all along," receiver Butch Johnson said. "The man can play quarterback."

Fortunately for Dallas, White showed that in the season opener.

"With the controversies that were brewing and the hard feelings that existed within the team," Pearson said, "I shudder to think what would have happened if we had lost that game. I definitely don't think we would have been on the roll that we were on.

"Winning makes you forget a lot."

COWBOYS 31, REDSKINS 30

	1	2	3	4	TOTAL
COWBOYS	0	3	14	14	31
REDSKINS	10	13	0	7	30

◆ FIRST QUARTER
W - Moseley FG 23, W 3-0
W - Riggins 1 run (Moseley kick), W 10-0
◆ SECOND QUARTER
D - Septien 26 FG, W 10-3
W - Moseley 30 FG, W 13-3
W - Moseley 39 FG, W 16-3
W - Brown 41 pass from Theismann (Moseley kick), W 23-3
◆ THIRD QUARTER
D - Hill 75 pass from White (Septien kick), W 23-10
D - Hill 51 pass from White (Septien kick), W 23-17
◆ FOURTH QUARTER
D - White 1 run (Septien kick), D 24-23
D - Cosbie 1 pass from White (Septien kick), D 31-23
W - Warren 1 pass from Theismann (Moseley kick), D 31-30

The Hogs

Respect piled high for the Doomsday Defense, particularly from the young Hogs. They knew first-hand of the Dallas defensive line's success. That didn't mean, however, that Washington's offensive linemen were awed by their counterparts.

They couldn't afford to be. Not with so much riding on their twice-yearly matchups with the Cowboys.

The core of the line was formed in 1981 and dubbed the Hogs the following training camp by line coach Joe Bugel. Mark May, Joe Jacoby, Russ Grimm and Jeff Bostic, all of whom came into the league after 1980, played to- gether from 1981 to 1989. Jacoby, Grimm and Bostic played into the 90s, winning three Super Bowls together.

From 1983-89, the Hogs combined for 10 Pro Bowl appearances. In 1983, the Redskins be- came the first team to place three linemen — Grimm, Bostic and Jacoby — in the Pro Bowl.

"We were a bunch of young punks coming in with this name and [the Doomsday line] didn't enjoy it," Jacoby said. "If we didn't play well, they would say, 'You're not so big and bad now are you?' They weren't real keen about [the nickname]."

Even the coaches got involved. After the national anthem at the 1982 NFC Championship Game, Bugel shouted across the field to Dallas defensive line coach Ernie Stautner. And flashed an obscene gesture.

That game increased the Hogs' fame as they dominated up front. Late in their 31-17 victory, the linemen even began telling Dallas All-Pro tackle Randy White that they were running at him. They did so nine straight plays.

Most of the line battles were civil. After all, they had to play versus one another for most of the 1980s. But May was different. He disliked White and

didn't hide it. Funny thing was, they rarely, if ever, lined up against one another.

Their animosity began in May's first game versus Dallas on Sept. 6, 1981. May, at left tackle play- ing against chatterbox end Harvey Martin, said White shoved him from behind after one play.

Thus, a rivalry developed.

"If he was by a pile, I'd pick him off," May said. "It got so bad the first year that I'd come back to the sidelines and the players were there waving to me because [White] would follow me after third downs. Then I'd turn around and he'd stand there on the hashmark and flip me the bird. He was Randy White, the Manster, and he wasn't going to take this from a rookie. And I was like, 'Screw him. He doesn't sign my pay- check.' "

Grimm, who played opposite White, said, "Mark would always be yapping at Randy and I would say, 'Keep your mouth shut! He's playing over me!' "

Once during the mid-80s, White and May represented their teams at an NFL drug seminar. When White entered the room, one chair remained open. It was next to May. White stood.

After one game, White told reporters that he couldn't stand May and would meet him anywhere to fight. Others said White told him during the game, "Meet me in the parking lot!"

"He didn't tell me that," May said. "Then after his little [butt has] gone away, that's when I hear about it."

A 1997 meeting was more civil. They ran into one another in the New Orleans airport before the Super Bowl.

"I saw him and thought, 'OK, here we go, right in the airport,' " May said. "But it was very good. Very civil, like we were friends forever. I guess time heals all wounds. Even with the Cowboys."

Doomsday Defense

Dallas' Doomsday defensive line had witnessed plenty long before the Hogs arrived. Its members combined for eight Pro Bowls before Washington's most famous offensive linemen even reached the NFL.

But the Hogs still provided a shock in their first meeting.

Midway through the 1981 season opener, 6-foot-7 tackle Joe Jacoby entered the game. Jacoby weighed 300 pounds at a time when that was uncommon.

"Randy White turns around and here's Joe Jacoby, he's a monster man," recalled Dallas defensive end Harvey Martin. "White says, 'My God, whose man is that?' And I go, 'Mine Randy, shut up!' Jacoby was a handful. He revolutionized offensive tackle."

Jacoby noticed the astonished glances in that first encounter.

"Harvey's just looking up and down at me," he said. "He didn't know what to do."

That rarely happened for the Doomsday line, which, in its heyday, consisted of Martin (end), White (tackle), Ed "Too Tall" Jones (end) and John Dutton (tackle). They combined for 16 Pro Bowls, including nine by Hall of Famer White, and three Super Bowl appearances.

Martin, White and Jones played together from 1975-83 until Martin retired.

"They were the players you had heard of through college," said Washington guard Mark May, who was part of the line group which came together in 1981 and a year later was dubbed the Hogs. "If you wanted to be the best, you had to beat them up. It couldn't be a fluke. You had to take the ball and ram it down their throats."

Typically these trench battles often decided the victor. In 1981 and 1982, Dallas won three straight from Washington. But the Redskins won four of the next five, including the 1982 NFC Championship Game which May said, "closed the door on the Doomsday Defense and opened the door on the Hogs."

Dallas sought answers for that passing of the torch.

"The Redskins do an excellent job of shoving and holding," Dallas defensive line coach Ernie Stautner said before a 1983 game. "The rules make it easy to hold. But they do a good job of it and we'll have to do our best to tear away from them."

On the field, the players usually remained silent.

Except for May and Martin.

"I hated him," Martin said of May. "He just wasn't that good of a guard, always running his mouth like he was going to do something good and he wouldn't.

"I talked noise all day long, and backed it up. Some days I'd get them and some days they'd get me. Yeah, I talked plenty of noise, but it helped me play better. I'd work myself up into a fevered pitch . . . and it would be great."

But Washington right tackle George Starke, nicknamed Head Hog, countered, "The real warriors never say anything. The only people that speak are afraid."

photo by Arnie Sachs/Consolidated News Pictures

And Redskins guard Fred Dean, still steamed about Martin tossing a wreath into the Redskins' locker room following Dallas' last-minute win in 1979, said, "Harvey had his big mouth, but he wasn't strong. We had no fear of Harvey. We feared Randy and Too Tall. They brought something to the party."

In the end, though, the Hogs understood the situation.

"These guys, whether you could stand them or not, were excellent players," said Washington tight end Doc Walker, an original Hog. "They had every reason to strut their stuff. It was up to us to knock them off the hill."

photo courtesy of the Washington Redskins

Washington's Alvin Garrett, Doc Walker, Otis Wonsley and Charlie Brown, as well as half their teammates, made more than just a fashion statement in 1983 with their army garb.

Dec. 11, 1983

Road Warriors

Redskins 31, Cowboys 10

They invaded Dallas, overwhelming the city and, a day later, the Cowboys. A platoon of 25 or so Washington Redskins decked in battle fatigues and black combat boots led the charge. They armed themselves with attitude.

Stares greeted them in the Dallas airport. Local media swarmed the Redskins' hotel, eager for pictures. Never before had a team traveled to a city for such a big game — with a division title and home field advantage at stake — carrying such bravado.

Their act dominated the Dallas television news that night. Word had spread among some Cowboys players. A few had heard that all the Redskins and even the coaches donned the fatigues.

Of course, the coaches had nothing to do with this. Imagine Washington coach Joe Gibbs wearing a camouflage outfit. But what the players wanted was his approval.

They weren't sure that would happen. After all, this was a coach who feared becoming bulletin-board fodder. That's why many players packed alternative travel outfits, just in case.

Gibbs, though, didn't discover the fashion statement until the players boarded the bus at Redskin Park for the ride to nearby Dulles Airport.

"If they had told me, I probably would have tried to talk them out of it," Gibbs said. "I was afraid that it would give the Cowboys something to get fired up about. But our guys had made up their minds that they were going to do it."

Not that Gibbs' displeasure didn't show.

"He looked like, 'I don't believe it, but I'm not going to overreact,'" tight end Doc Walker recalled. "I looked at the assistant coaches, especially the guys who had played the game and they had all been through this. You could sense that they were like, 'You guys have [guts].'"

Or, as Washington guard Russ Grimm said, "I imagine that Joe was about ready to throw up."

But the Redskins were ready for this game. For three months they had waited to wash a bitter taste from their mouths, a 31-30 loss to the Cowboys in the season opener. Lest anyone forget, Dallas had

rallied from a 23-3 halftime deficit. Washington hadn't forgotten.

Since that game, the Cowboys had lost to the Los Angeles Raiders and San Diego by a combined three points while the Redskins had lost, 48-47, to Green Bay. Two points, two losses.

And there was the matter of home field advantage as well as the NFC East championship as both teams entered with 12-2 records. It was only the second time division rivals had won 12 games in the same season since the NFL-AFL merger in 1969.

That's why about two dozen Redskins ventured to a Washington area Army surplus store to buy their fatigues. Some, such as Grimm, already owned this garb. Grimm also carried a dud hand grenade while linebacker Neal Olkewicz toted a commando bag.

No one recalls the idea's exact genesis. Surely, though, it stemmed from Olkewicz and running back John Riggins, who had donned a combat helmet before practices that week.

"Riggo didn't care what anybody thought," said Charley Casserly, then the Redskins' assistant general manager.

It was a gutsy move considering Washington hadn't won in Dallas since 1976 and was 1-9 there in the past 10 years. But this time, the clothes made the man. Or men.

"It showed our mindset," Olkewicz said. "We honestly felt like we were going into battle."

Turns out the battle at Texas Stadium was one-sided. It even caused disintegration among the Dallas troops. There was quarterback Danny White audibilizing on a fourth-down play designed simply to draw Washington offside. The Redskins stuffed the play. There were defensive backs Dennis Thurman and Michael Downs interrupting the Fun Bunch end zone celebration. And there was running back Tony Dorsett picking a fight with defensive tackle Darryl Grant.

"A lot of times stuff like that happens when you're getting your butts kicked," Dorsett said. "You resort to other measures."

While the camouflaged outfits grabbed the headlines, Washington's execution won the game. Dallas' offense sputtered, despite playing against a secondary dubbed, "The Pearl Harbor Crew" for its weekly bombings.

But the Redskins held the Cowboys to 173 yards passing — and a backup safety who had played just eight snaps all season, Greg Williams, intercepted two passes. And Dallas managed only a franchise-low 33 yards rushing on 20 carries.

It's no wonder the Cowboys scored fewer than 21 points for the first time that year.

Washington defensive tackle Dave Butz, who did not wear the fatigues, dominated up front. He sacked White three times for minus-25 yards.

Then there was the Redskins' offense. In the first meeting, Dallas had often blitzed its safeties, plugging the middle. To defeat that strategy, Gibbs started three receivers rather than two. That took a safety from the middle and, if the Cowboys wanted to blitz, they would have to give it away by walking toward the line.

Also, Washington ran Riggins from three- and four-receiver sets. Whether all of this was the difference, the Redskins rolled from the start.

"I'll always remember this game because we came up with a few things technically," Gibbs said. "It was one of our better game plans. I never thought much about the fatigues once we started playing."

Washington scored on its first two drives, opening a 14-0 lead. A 27-yard pass interference penalty on safety Downs gave Washington a first down at the Dallas 7. Two plays later, Riggins scored from the 3.

Riggins helped set up the second score without touching the ball. Quarterback Joe Theismann play-faked to Riggins, causing safety Dextor Clinkscale to fall. That left tight end Clint Didier wide open for a 40-yard touchdown.

But, as in the season opener, Dallas rallied. The comeback began after Riggins was stuffed on fourth-and-inches from the Washington 48 — the Redskins entered the game 9 for 10 on fourth-down plays. Two plays later, White hit tight end Doug Cosbie for a 29-yard touchdown with 37 seconds left in the first quarter.

Rafael Septien capped a 49-yard drive with a 35-yard field goal 49 seconds before halftime, narrowing the gap to 14-10.

Then came the real adventure for the Redskins. On the first drive of the second half, Dallas had a fourth-and-1 from its 49 and attempted to draw Washington offside.

White had other ideas, however. He audibilized to a handoff for running back Ron Springs. Once center Tom Rafferty heard the call, he dissented.

"No! No! No! Don't run that play!" Butz remembered hearing Rafferty shout.

"That was the first time I'd heard a center absolutely refuse to continue on with the play," Butz said. "You just say to yourself with a little bit of glee, 'Oh good!' "

On the sidelines, usually-stoic coach Tom Landry shouted, "No! No! No, Danny!"

But, Butz said White told Rafferty to keep quiet and run the play. Bad choice. Springs was nailed by Olkewicz and Mann, among others, for a 2-yard loss.

"Danny seemed intent on creating his own tempo," Dallas receiver Drew Pearson said, "or his own place in Cowboy history. Danny wanted to be the cerebral quarterback. Even though Landry would call a play, he wanted to outsmart Landry by calling something different."

The Dallas defense held after the fourth-down mishap and, one series later, Downs intercepted Theismann on the goal line.

That's the last time the ball bounced the Cowboys' way. On their next series, White's pass skipped off Cosbie's hands into Pearson's at the Dallas 35. But cornerback Vernon Dean nailed Pearson, popping the ball into the air. Rookie cornerback Darrell Green snagged it before falling to the ground at the 43.

Next play: Theismann to receiver Art Monk, beating reserve cornerback Ron Fellows, for a touchdown and a 21-10 lead.

The Fun Bunch, a group of Redskins, gathered for their usual touchdown celebration, a mass leap-

Dallas has played better on the road in this series than Washington. The Cowboys are 17-21 in the nation's capital, including two postseason defeats, while the Redskins are 11-22-2 in Texas.

ing and high-fiving. Downs and cornerback Thurman had other ideas. They broke into this circle, trying to prevent a celebration on their turf, something they had talked about in practice that week. They only got in the way.

"I remember saying to Thurman, 'Save your energy for the play,'" said Walker, the originator of the Fun Bunch. "They were clearly disrupted. They should have exerted some of that energy to stop Art."

Thurman said, "Not only do they beat us, but they were always embarrassing us and humiliating us. I mean, come on, let's be professional here. It was something that was always on our minds to do and we did it and we ended up looking bad. But the NFL ended up changing the [end zone celebration] rule, so maybe we weren't so bad."

Fellows had a more succinct reason for why it happened.

"We got tired of that crap," he said.

Though the game was still close, the Cowboys' cool had melted in front of 65,074 fans. Dorsett proved that early in the fourth.

He caught a screen pass and turned it into a 13-yard gain. Defensive tackle Darryl Grant and Williams tackled him from behind. Dorsett and Grant exchanged shoves on the way up and Dorsett whipped the ball at Grant's helmet.

Dorsett was ticked because he said someone had drilled a knee into his back. Perhaps his 34 yards on 14 carries to this point contributed as well.

"Before I realized what I did, I slammed the ball at his forehead," Dorsett said. "I was like, 'Oh, [shoot]!' I looked at the size of him and said, 'Oh, boy!' I'm on national TV, I can't just take off and run so I have to stand here like a man and bring it on. He decided not to do anything and I was so happy.

"But you talk about throwing a strike. I hit him dead smack in the center. Bam. I hit him and that ball took off. That was a great throw. If I tried it for 100 years, I couldn't throw it any better."

The Redskins didn't like Dorsett — they considered him too mouthy, though they would talk back. Grant said they didn't like that after be-

ing tackled, Dorsett would get up and sometimes flip the ball in the defender's face.

They enjoyed nothing more than smacking into No. 33. But when Grant had the chance, he wisely backed away as others intervened. Dorsett was nailed with a 15-yard penalty.

"It increased the intensity of the game," Grant recalled.

After Dorsett's penalty, with Dallas facing a first-and-27 from its 44, Williams intercepted White and returned the ball 25 yards. Two plays later, a 37-yard pass interference penalty on cornerback Rod Hill, covering Receiver Charlie Brown, gave Washington a first down at the 4. On fourth-and-1, Riggins bulled over for the touchdown and 28-10 lead with 11:19 remaining.

Williams' second interception led to the game's final three points.

The Cowboys sputtered in the playoffs. After losing the regular-season finale, they were eliminated by the Los Angeles Rams in the first round. The Redskins easily advanced to their second straight Super Bowl, where they lost to the Raiders, 38-9. Despite the ending, many Redskins considered this their best team.

They mixed a confident arrogance with talent. And no day typified that more than Dec. 11.

The battle fatigues were retired after this win. But the memory of the invasion survived.

"Thank God we won," Olkewicz said. "We never would have lived that down."

Instead, they'll never forget it. As Redskins offensive tackle Joe Jacoby said, "Mission accomplished."

REDSKINS 31, COWBOYS 10

	1	2	3	4	TOTAL
REDSKINS	14	0	7	10	31
COWBOYS	7	3	0	0	10

◆ **FIRST QUARTER**
W - Riggins 3 run (Moseley kick), W 7-0
W - Didier 40 pass from Theismann (Moseley kick), W 14-0
D - Cosbie 29 pass from White (Septien kick), W 14-7

◆ **SECOND QUARTER**
D - Septien 35 FG, W 14-10

◆ **THIRD QUARTER**
W - Monk 43 pass from Theismann (Moseley kick), W 21-10

◆ **FOURTH QUARTER**
W - Riggins 1 run (Moseley kick), W 28-10
W - Moseley 38 FG, W 31-10

Dallas running back Tony Dorsett and his teammates picked apart Washington in 1985.

Sept. 9, 1985

'Thieves' Steal Joe's Day

Cowboys 44, Redskins 14

And they all began to sing as one, the remainder of the 62,292 fans in Texas Stadium, their hearts and soul on this Monday night leading them in sarcastic needling and therapeutic venting.

For them, this was a long time coming.

Oh, how they sang, "Happy birthday to you, happy birthday to you, HAP-py BIRTH-day to JOE-oh, happy birthday to you."

They robustly applauded themselves, knowing as bad a night as it had been for Washington Redskins quarterback Joe Theismann, having thrown five interceptions on national TV while losing this 1985 season opener, 44-14, to the Dallas Cowboys, his 36th birthday had just grown significantly worse. The nerve, he must have thought.

"Joey was the perfect Redskin," said Cowboys receiver Drew Pearson, who attended South River (N.J.) High School with Theismann, which is why to this day he calls him Joey. "He hated the Cowboys. He was an instigating type guy, always running his mouth. So that year, that game, we were rubbing it in pretty good. But we didn't care. That's the way it was back then."

Theismann got his all right, as far as the Cowboys were concerned, because this game was more than five interceptions or Dallas' worst beating of Washington since 1970 or the most points the Cowboys had scored on the Redskins since hanging 45 on them in 1970. This was revenge, in part for the Redskins having won the past two NFC East titles and having played in two of the past three Super Bowls. And in part for having won four of the past five meetings, including that 1982 NFC Championship Game.

But this also was about exorcising some Texas-sized hostility that had been building since Theismann took over as the Redskins' starting quarterback in 1978. He first taunted them while taking a game-ending safety that year in a 9-5 victory, and this hostility toward the former Notre Dame quarterback absolutely exploded in the second meeting of 1984, a 30-28 Washington victory that all but ended the Cowboys' streak of nine consecutive playoff appearances.

In fact, the game clock at Texas Stadium that 9th day of December, 1984, never did expire. Referee Tom Dooley called a judicious halt to the proceedings with 24 seconds remaining when a brawl broke out on the field, one Cowboys cornerback Ron Fellows said was "about

to be a baseball, clear-the-dugout kind of deal."

Fellows should know. He lit the fuse.

That game was basically over. The Redskins had their 30-28 lead, the ball at the Cowboys 28 and the clock ticking down from 1:17. Dallas had no timeouts. NFL protocol called for Theismann to kneel on the Cowboys, letting them stew as their own clock ran out.

He did so the first time, fine.

He kneeled again on second down, but realized no one had touched him, and as Washington coach Joe Gibbs later would say in his defense, Theismann got up to run around a little more, presumably to run more time off the clock. The Redskins certainly did not want to attempt a field goal.

"Well, when he came around the end, there was no one out there but me," Fellows said, "because even his running backs didn't know what he was doing because he was back there running around. And instead of me just knocking the crap out of him, I just grabbed him."

Now 41 seconds remained. Theismann was going to kneel again.

"We had some crazy guys," admitted Cowboys safety Dennis Thurman, who claimed there was no sinister plot hatched in the huddle between plays. "We all dealt with the rivalry in our own way. But it was always a personal deal, always."

Fellows went ahead and dealt.

"I used to be on the field-goal block team, so I was used to coming in there and diving all the time," Fellows said of the third down play. "So I said to myself, 'OK, I'll get [him].' And then, man, he kneeled down again and started to get up."

Fellows went crashing through, landing on Theismann, causing fists, flags and tempers to go flying.

"I said to him, 'Now get up and do it again,' " Fellows remembered.

Redskins 295-pound tackle Mark May was the first to grab Fellows. Then Cowboys defensive tackle Randy White, who never had any love lost for the Redskins, snatched May. They began to sumo wrestle, as all hell broke lose.

"I was one of the first out on the field," said Cowboys 175-pound receiver Mike Renfro. "I dove out there into the pile like some decathlon athlete high jumping. Right in the middle of that sucker, and I remember getting about a $1,000 fine."

Peace never could be restored, and in the middle of this mayhem Cowboys defensive tackle John Dutton remembers White screaming at May, as the two were being pulled apart, "Meet me in the parking lot after the game," and re-enacting the scene the next Monday at the Cowboys' training facility much to his own delight.

"Joe Theismann is a garbage-mouth little SOB," Dutton said after the game. "He's such a hot dog that all he needs is the bun. He's got absolutely no class."

White echoed the sentiment, saying, "He's nothing but a damn hot dog. He's a hot dog and a showboat and I hate him."

So there, how about that for hostility?

The bitterness escalated going into the 1985 season opener when a letter to the editor was printed by the *Cowboys Weekly*, ostensibly from a Tom Whidby of Vienna, Va., claiming at Theismann's restaurant opening that summer the Cowboys antagonist was saying such things as:

"The Cowboys' key players are over the hill."

"[Dallas quarterback] Danny White panicked."

"You could see in their eyes they were choking."

"They'll finish fifth [in the East]."

Persistent questions about the final seconds of the 1984 game, combined with the Cowboys continuing to rag on Theismann that week of the 1985 opener apparently lit Gibbs' fuse. The Washington coach went out of his way on Thursday to defend Theismann's honor, explaining how if Theismann had continued to simply kneel, the clock never would have expired.

Then Gibbs, totally out of character, sent a rebuttal to that letter to the editor. Gibbs' response ran in the Fort Worth Star-Telegram alongside the original letter the day of the game.

Gibbs made several points: Theismann had not opened a "new" restaurant; police could find no records of a Tom Whidby in Vienna; the remarks themselves were "ludicrous"; and that "if there is a Mr. Whidby, would he kindly step forward so blame can be pointed in the right direction."

All this for a football game.

"Well everyone on our defense wanted [Theismann]," remembered Cowboys running back Tony Dorsett. "They probably still want to get Joe the way he ran his mouth. They wanted to knock him out cold."

They might as well have.

The Cowboys, with the help of secondary coach Gene Stallings, devised a somewhat different defense to handle the Redskins' three-receivers. They employed an extra defensive back on their standard defense, using safety Bill Bates as a linebacker in a version of the nickel. This not only allowed the Cowboys to cover the Redskins' three receivers, but it also caused confusion for Washington's running game.

"It changed up who to block, how to block, and now the big ol' Hogs were chasing these guys who were faster and quicker," Thurman said. "To them it was like, shoot, we can't run the ball and we can't throw the ball, either."

Still, the Redskins were hanging tough, despite rushing for only 43 yards the first half and Cowboys free safety Michael Downs picking off a Theismann pass. Hanging tough, that is, until Renfro, of modest speed, burned Darrell Green, soon to become known as the "NFL's Fastest Man," with time running out on a 10-7 first half.

"I ran a curl pattern, and Danny made a nice pump fake," said Renfro, who would finish the day with five catches for 99 yards. "Darrell bit, and I just went on by him. But I'll tell you the funny thing about it: On film, when Danny throws the ball, I'm real close when I say I was seven yards beyond Darrell. I didn't break stride to catch the ball, which means I didn't slow down for the ball. And by the time the ball got to my hands, Darrell Green is in full extension, trying to reach up at the last minute to tip the ball away. I'll never forget how fast Darrell is."

Opening days and Monday nights have mixed well with Dallas. The Cowboys are 29-21 on Monday Night Football and 27-9-1 in Week 1. The Redskins are 22-21 on Monday nights and 28-29-3 in season openers. Head-to-head, Dallas leads the Week 1 battle, 5-1-1, but Washington has the upper hand on Monday night, 5-4.

To remind himself of that momentous occasion, Renfro, whose dad Ray once coached for the Redskins, has a picture of that play on a wall at home.

The 55-yard touchdown with just six seconds remaining in the half gave the Cowboys a 17-7 lead. The flood gates opened on Theismann following halftime.

First Washington possession: Everson Walls intercepted Theisman, setting up a 39-yard Rafael Septien field goal.

Second possession: Strong safety Dextor Clinkscale recovered a fumble by running back George Rogers which had been forced by linebacker Eugene Lockhart, setting up a 43-yard Septien field goal for a 23-7 Cowboys lead.

Third possession: Fellows intercepted Theismann. "I had hurt my knee, but I went back out there until I got me one, then went and sat down," Fellows said– setting up Dorsett's 9-yard touchdown run to make it 30-7.

Fifth possession: Bates picked off Theismann.

Second possession, fourth quarter: defensive back Victor Scott intercepted Theismann, returning the ball 26 yards for a touchdown and a 37-7 lead with 9:29 left to play.

And then just for good measure, after Washington finally had scored a second touchdown, cutting the margin to 37-14 on Theismann's 19-yard pass to tight end Clint Didier, Thurman himself picked one, the fifth Cowboys' interception. He, too, returned the ball for a touchdown, this one for 21 yards.

Theismann, who completed just 15-of-35 passes for 206 yards, mercifully was replaced by Jay Schroeder the next, and final possession.

"We were working so damn long for these guys, maybe we got a little stale," Theismann said. "We started working on this game six weeks ago, and I'm damn glad it's over with. Enough already."

Not for the Cowboys, who still gloat over that night.

"The culmination of a great evening," said Thurman, whose four career interception returns for touchdowns remains a Cowboys record.

Thus the inception of "Thurman's Thieves," so named by Danny White, a moniker the Cowboys' defensive backs would carry all season. The distinction actually caused a slight rift on the team when "Thurman's Thieves" did a live television interview before a Monday night game in St. Louis wearing the gangster-type hats they had bought in a mall.

This group, though – Thurman, Walls, Fellows, Downs, Scott, Bates and Clinkscale – was a big reason for the Cowboys' success in 1985, and certainly in this season opener.

"I remember Joe sitting over on the sideline with his face in his palms," Thurman said. "It was a great moment for us players who had been in that rivalry such a long time. To have a blowout in a game like that, that has so much personal emotion to it, it was a great beginning to a season."

The Redskins would abdicate the NFC East to the Cowboys this year, even losing the rematch, 13-7, the first time Dallas had swept the two-game series since 1981. Washington would not even qualify for the playoffs, for the first time in four seasons. The Cowboys returned after their one-year absence, losing a first-round game to the Los Angeles Rams, 20-0 in their last playoff appearance until 1991.

"They were out for revenge, and they got us," Redskins tackle Joe Jacoby said.

Sure they were, the hostility having been pent up far too long, and why Theismann's 36th birthday had made so many others so very happy, especially those at Texas Stadium who were able to "properly" serenade him in the final minutes with that Happy Birthday chorus.

"It was great," Thurman said of hearing the crowd sing to Theismann. "It was awesome."

And so typical of this no-love-lost rivalry.

COWBOYS 44, REDSKINS 14

	1	2	3	4	TOTAL
REDSKINS	0	7	0	7	14
COWBOYS	3	14	13	14	44

◆ **FIRST QUARTER**
D - Septien 53 FG, D 3-0

◆ **SECOND QUARTER**
D - Newsome 1 run (Septien kick), D 10-0
W - Riggins 1 run (Moseley kick), D 10-7
D - Renfro 55 pass from White (Septien kick), D 17-7

◆ **THIRD QUARTER**
D - Septien 39 FG, D 20-7
D - Septien 43 FG, D 23-7
D - Dorsett 9 run (Septien kick), D 30-7

◆ **FOURTH QUARTER**
D - Scott 26 interception return (Septien kick), D 37-7
D - Didier 19 pass from Theismann (Moseley kick), D 37-14
D - Thurman 21 interception return (Septien kick), D 44-14

photo by Arnie Sachs/Consolidated News Pictures

Dallas quarterback Danny White, surrounded by unfamiliar players and rushed by the "Subskins", drops back to pass.

Oct. 19, 1987

Striking A Blow

Redskins 13, Cowboys 7

They came from everywhere. The Canadian Football League. 7-Eleven. Jail. Hardly any had been drafted. Most hadn't met a month before they carved their place in Washington Redskins history.

Call them replacement players or call them scabs. It doesn't matter. Those 60 or so nobodies pulled one of the NFL's most shocking upsets among their three straight victories to help propel the Redskins to the Super Bowl title a little over three months later.

Having endured a players' strike in 1982 which had cancelled seven weeks of the season, the NFL owners were ready if the players walked out with the expiration of the labor agreement in 1987. Spurred by Cowboys president Tex Schramm, the head of the league's competition committee, the owners were going to replace the regulars with castoffs and keep playing.

The NFL told each club it could offer "contracts" to players it cut during training camp, giving their exclusive rights to that club in case of a strike.

"Initially I said no," said offensive tackle Mark Carlson, who had been in Washington's training camp as a rookie free agent. "I had gotten really close with Russ Grimm, Joe Jacoby, Jeff Bostic and the rest of the Hogs. I didn't want to go against guys I really respected. But after talking to my agent and my dad and I figured, 'This is my one shot.' "

The strike started after Week 2. The next week's games were cancelled as the clubs scrambled to fill out their rosters to be ready for Week 4 in case the strike wasn't settled.

Eighteen replacement Redskins, including "contracted" guard Darrick Brilz and quarterback Ed Rubbert, had been in camp. A few others, such as defensive tackle Dan Benish, cornerback Dennis Woodberry and receiver Anthony Allen, had NFL experience.

In contrast, guard Willard Scissum was working as a 7-Eleven security guard. Tony Robinson had been a star quarterback at Tennessee before a drug problem landed him in jail. Safety Charles Jackson was such a student of geography that he said, "I'm proud to represent the state of Washington" after becoming a Redskin. Others had strong union backgrounds in their families, but opted to cross the picket line for the chance at stardom.

But after countless hours on the phone, Washington assistant general manager Charley Casserly still had just seven offensive linemen, including a snapper. Flipping through scouting books from April's draft, the Redskins found 6-foot-6, 290-pound Don Tucker from tiny Cal-State Northridge. Tucker arrived at Redskin Park so out of shape that climbing the stairs to Casserly's office exhausted him. But the desperate Redskins signed him anyway.

Tucker's teammates anticipated an equally rough welcome.

"Twelve of us flew on the same plane to Dulles Airport, but we didn't know who each other was," said defensive end Alec Gibson. "It was like a spy movie. There was a security guard waiting for us. They hustled us onto a bus to the hotel."

When the newcomers rode the bus to Redskin Park the next morning for their first day of meetings and practice, the veterans — every one of whom was honoring the walkout unlike those on several strike-torn teams — were waiting.

"There was definite fear," recalled replacement running back Lionel Vital. "You didn't know what they would do."

The veterans just wanted to prevent the bus from getting inside Redskin Park's boundaries, grab some attention and leave. But defensive tackle Darryl Grant was angry that so few of his teammates had shown up for the 7 a.m. protest.

"I jumped up and tried to swat the bus with an open palm to make some noise," Grant said. "I hit a window and it shattered. Cameramen and reporters were all over the place. The next thing I know, it's 'Violence erupts at Redskin Park.' "

Carlson, who was sitting near the shattered window, just laughed. The replacement players weren't going to be scared off.

Grant paid $800 to fix the bus. Thereafter, the front office snuck players in through the woods behind the practice fields.

"All of a sudden a new guy [ex-CFL linebacker

Jeff Braswell] shows up in the huddle," Casserly recalled. "Pecc [linebackers coach Larry Peccatiello] didn't know where he came from."

Redskins coach Joe Gibbs hadn't wanted to work with the replacements, but he soon appreciated their spirit.

"Usually I could go in to eat a hamburger on snack night because some of the guys would have gone out to eat, but these kids would eat everything that was standing," Gibbs said. "Just to see the unspoiled way they went after things was exciting."

But how could these rag-tag Redskins even think of beating the St. Louis Cardinals, who had 15 regulars, including receivers Roy Green and J.T. Smith, running backs Vai Sikahema and Earl Ferrell, defensive end Curtis Greer and linebacker E.J. Junior?

"I was scared to death before the first game," Casserly admitted. "I had no idea if we could score, let alone win."

But the "Subskins" won 28-21 as Rubbert passed for 334 yards and three touchdowns, all to Allen, whose 255 receiving yards set a club record.

"We were as well-prepared as any team because of Joe Gibbs," said tight end Craig McEwen, who remained a Redskin until the summer of 1989 and then spent three seasons with San Diego.

With their confidence surging, the replacements went to New York and romped, 38-12, as Vital ran for 128 yards and a touchdown while the defense held the Giants to 171 total yards.

"We couldn't understand why Lionel hadn't been in the pros," Gibson said. "He would lower his shoulder and run about a foot off the ground."

The "Subskins" were 2-0, but they couldn't possibly win in Dallas. With the strike ending after the Monday Night game at Texas Stadium, running back Tony Dorsett, defensive tackle Randy White (both Hall of Famers), defensive end Ed "Too Tall" Jones and quarterback Danny White were among the 11 veteran Cowboys who had rejoined the team by Wednesday's deadline.

"If it was basketball or another sport that's not quite as team-oriented, where you could play more one-on-one, then the veterans could make a difference," Danny White prophetically told The Dallas Times-Herald. "But you could have the greatest player in the world and if he's surrounded by 10 guys who have never played football, they aren't going to succeed."

Meanwhile, Washington's veterans had returned a day too late to be reinstated, setting up what seemed to be a gigantic mismatch.

Despite adding so many key regulars to a replace-

ment team which had pounded the New York Jets, 38-24, and Philadelphia, 41-22, Dallas coach Tom Landry was in a quandary.

"My feeling is, let's meet on even grounds, play the replacements and see what happens, but it's hard not to play the hand that's dealt you," Landry said.

And some of Landry's best cards didn't want to be in the deck.

"Tex told us if we didn't come back he would take our annuities," said Dorsett, one of the Cowboys who had such future payments in his contract. "I had 20 years worth. I didn't want to risk losing that, but I wasn't proud to be a Cowboy at that time. I'd go to practice and go back on the picket line. I didn't give a damn."

Even Schramm admitted, "We took the heart out [of the replacement team] when all of a sudden the other guys [the regulars] were in there."

Washington's other guys refused to be awestruck.

"It definitely helped going into Dallas having won those first two games," said Carlson, who spent the rest of season on injured reserve and never played another NFL game. "We had a lot of confidence even if they had Randy White and 'Too Tall', guys whose football cards I had as a kid, guys I had looked up to. I'll never forget [Washington offensive line coach] Joe Bugel telling Ed Rubbert in warmups to throw the ball at [Dallas defensive line coach] Ernie Stautner. It him in the shoulder. That showed me how much the Redskins hated the Cowboys."

Gibbs helped calm nerves with a rousing pre-game talk.

"We were pretty nervous," Brilz said. "We knew Dallas had some big-name players. But Gibbs loosened us up. He said, 'We've got nothing to lose. They should win. But we're going to.'"

Gibbs also stressed what the game could do for the players.

"Joe said, 'People are saying it's too bad you've got to play Dallas down here on Monday Night,'" Casserly recalled. "He said, 'This is what you want. You want to be able to out on national television and show 26 other teams that you can play in this league. This is your final audition.'"

That audition began with great promise for the "Subskins." On the game's sixth snap, Gibson slapped the ball away from Dorsett. Benish recovered at the Dallas 46.

"Dorsett cut it up instead of going outside," remembered Gibson, whose career ended in the Arena League in 1988. "I lost my balance, but as I did, I reached my hand across his arm and I guess I knocked the ball out. When they told me what had happened,

I was as surprised as anyone."

So was White when Brilz knocked him down on Washington's second play.

"Randy got up and spit in my face and said, 'You can't block me kid,' " Brilz said. "I said, 'Yes I can.' "

With Rubbert finding tight end Joe Caravello for 22 yards, Brilz and the Redskins drove to the Cowboys' 1. However, fullback Wayne Wilson was thrown for a loss on third-and-goal so Obed Ariri kicked a 19-yard field goal.

Washington defensive end Steve Martin helped ruin Dallas' second series by sacking Danny White. Gibson ended the third by forcing another Dorsett fumble which linebacker Bobby Curtis recovered at the Dallas 41. The 60,415 Cowboys fans began to boo Dorsett and White.

"When I made the choice to go with Danny and Dorsett, I was committed," Landry said. "I had to stick with the veterans. It was their game to win or lose."

Rubbert left the game with a bruised shoulder after being hit by linebacker Dale Jones, but Robinson came in and drove Washington to the 5.

"When Ed got hurt, I thought we were in big trouble because Tony hadn't played at all, but Tony came in all cool, calm and collected," McEwen said. "It was just like practice."

However, the drive ended when Vital fumbled and Cowboys defensive tackle Kevin Brooks recovered. Linebacker Carlton Rose's sack — one of six White endured in the first half — and safety Steve Gage's tackle of Dorsett for a 5-yard loss on a screen pass stopped Dallas yet again.

Vital's 21-yard burst set up Ariri from 43 yards, but the kick hit the right goalpost. When Washington got the ball back, Vital ran for 29 yards. The Redskins then tricked Randy White into jumping offside on fourth-and-2 at the 16. However, White atoned by sacking Robinson and then pressuring him into a bad throw which safety Tommy Haynes intercepted. So it was still 3-0, Redskins, at halftime.

"We were disappointed we weren't up by more because we had really been outplaying them," Brilz said.

That feeling only intensified in the second half. Robinson connected with McEwen for 42 yards on the first play of the third quarter. Vital then carried three times for 17 of his 136 yards and McEwen followed with a 6-yard grab (one of his seven catches for 108 yards) on third-and-4. Brilz was flagged for holding, but on first-and-

goal from the 16, receiver Teddy Wilson scooted around left end for the touchdown. David led Goliath, 10-0.

"We wanted to show the country that we had a good team and this was our chance to do that," said Vital, who would catch on with Buffalo that season and Detroit in 1988 before heading to the CFL. "This was our reward night."

The Cowboys responded with a seven-play, 80-yard drive finished off by Danny White's 38-yard scoring pass to receiver Kelvin Edwards. Washington kept the ball for the next seven minutes, but on second-and-goal from the Dallas 12, Haynes picked off Robinson once more. However, the Cowboys went nowhere and Ariri's 38-yard field goal concluded a 13-play march that consumed 7:04. With 6:13 remaining, the Redskins were on top 13-7.

Cornerback Mike Mitchell intercepted White four plays later when Edwards didn't hear the audible and ran inside instead of outside, but the Cowboys didn't quit. Backed up to his 3 with a little over 2:00 left, White hit six straight passes. Dallas was on the Washington 20 with 50 seconds to go, but on fourth-and-3 from the 14, Edwards couldn't hold White's high pass at the 5.

The "Subskins" had done the unthinkable. The stunned Cowboys would go into a tailspin and wind up at 7-8, their first losing season in 23 years.

"It was embarassing," said veteran Dallas receiver Mike Renfro.

"We had no continuity," Landry lamented. "We didn't have any fire."

The Redskins hugged and laughed even though most knew their football careers were over. Brilz, who would be the only "Subskin" to remain active in the 1990s, was so drained that he almost passed out.

"It was one of my greatest experiences and wins," Gibbs said. "It was kind of like a miracle."

REDSKINS 13, COWBOYS 7

	1	2	3	4	TOTAL
REDSKINS	3	0	7	3	13
COWBOYS	0	0	7	0	7

◆ **FIRST QUARTER**
W - Ariri 19 FG, W 3-0

◆ **THIRD QUARTER**
W - T. Wilson 16 run (Ariri kick), W 10-0
D - Edwards 38 pass from D. White (Brady kick), W 10-7

◆ **FOURTH QUARTER**
W - Ariri 39 FG, W 13-7

Joe Gibbs

In the beginning, Jimmy Johnson was just trying to find his way in the NFL and Joe Gibbs, with two Super Bowl titles under his belt and former Cowboys coach Tom Landry out of his hair, was just going about his business.

"My burning desire from the time I was a young kid was to compete and beat somebody," said Gibbs, who added a national senior racquetball title and a Daytona 500 triumph as an owner to the three Super Bowl trophies he won with the Redskins.

And despite the Cowboys' slide in the late 1980s and the ascendance of the New York Giants and Philadelphia Eagles in the NFC East, the Dallas games were usually as huge during Gibbs' tenure (1981-92) as they were under emotional former Washington coach George Allen (1971-77).

"It was the Cowboys and the Indians," Gibbs said. "Everybody was on one side or the other. There were times with

photo courtesy of the Washington Redskins

Buddy Ryan in Philadelphia that was an intense hate and there were times when things were going with Bill Parcells and the Giants, but overall, it was Dallas and Washington. It was ingrained in me that you have to beat Dallas. That's why I consider one of my greatest victories the [1982] NFC Championship Game when we beat Dallas at our place right before our first Super Bowl."

Gibbs was just 40 when he came to Washington for his first had coaching job. Dallas coach Tom Landry was 56 and had already been to five Super Bowls, winning two.

"I was probably a little intimidated at first," said Gibbs, who lost his first three games against his fellow Hall of Famer. "I pictured him as a football genius."

But Gibbs beat Landry in their final four meetings to even their record at 8-8. Then the Cowboys replaced the taciturn Landry with the brash Jimmy Johnson, who had never coached an NFL game. Now Gibbs was the veteran with two Super Bowl trophies.

"I wouldn't think Jimmy was ever intimidated going against me the way I was going against Landry," said Gibbs, who retired in 1993. "I had great respect for the way Jimmy put that thing together from nothing. I looked at Jimmy as an extremely talented personnel guy. He wasn't the technical X's and O's guy Landry was. But he was also a different kind of motivator."

Gibbs, who now comments for NBC on Johnson's coaching in Miami, will only admit that the rivalry was more personal with Johnson than it was with Landry. But ex-Redskins know better.

"I don't think Joe really cared for Jimmy, his cockiness, his arrogance," said Jeff Bostic, Gibbs' center for 12 years.

"Jimmy said, 'Give me a handful of guys and I'll build a team around them,' " explained defensive end Charles Mann, who played 10 years for Gibbs. "Joe said, 'Give me a team.' Jimmy wanted superstars. Joe wanted regular folks."

Just like him.

Jimmy Johnson

In the beginning, Jimmy Johnson was just trying to find his way in the NFL and Joe Gibbs, with two Super Bowl titles under his belt and former coach Tom Landry out of his hair, was just going about his business.

No animosity existed between Gibbs and Johnson. Yet, that is. After all, this was Dallas-Washington, so no player, no coach was immune from the malignant bitterness that somehow infects all participants.

At least Johnson and Gibbs had a chance. They had crossed paths during their assistant coaching days in college.

"Joe and I worked together there at Arkansas, so I had known him for a long time," Johnson said of their brief association at his alma mater.

Still, familiarity is no cure for this Cowboys-Redskins malice.

So it began almost immediately when Johnson inherited a 3-13 Dallas team in 1989, and promptly stripped it to the barest of essentials. And when the two coaches met for a second time that year, the 0-8 Cowboys were trying to avoid the first 0-16 season in the NFL. The 4-4 Redskins were trying to recapture the form that had earned them the Super Bowl title two years earlier. Dallas beat Washington 13-3 that Sunday night at RFK Stadium, for its only victory of the season.

The two coaches would split every year they matched up. In 1991, the Cowboys' victory — 24-21 at RFK in Game 12 — ended Washington's bid to become the NFL's first 16-0 team. And if that were not enough to create animosity, the Redskins delayed the Cowboys' run at the NFC East title in 1992, beating them 20-17 at RFK in Game 14 when a Dallas victory could have clinched the division.

"Just talking to some of the Redskins' coaches over the years, they always felt like Joe was so con-

photo courtesy of the Dallas Cowboys

cerned about the Cowboys, sometimes they were out of whack when they went into the game," Johnson said. "For one reason or another, both teams have played different from what they normally had played."

Needless to say Johnson's ways were different, too, especially the way he formed a team and treated his players. Former Cowboys wide receiver Alvin Harper, now with the Redskins, can attest to that.

"I thought about giving back the money and quitting my first training camp with Jimmy," Harper said. "I couldn't believe how hard he made us work. Two-a-days for four straight weeks where we were really hitting. But I knew I wanted to play in the pros, so I stayed. And pretty soon I saw how all that hard work paid off. Teams could stay with us for maybe two or three quarters, but in the fourth quarter, our conditioning paid off. An 80-yard drive would seem like a 10-yard drive."

Funny, though, once the Cowboys began to win under Johnson, going back-to-back in Super Bowls XXVII and XXVIII and starting a streak of five consecutive NFC East titles, his perception among the Redskins began to change.

"Before it was the Dallas Cowboys, and now it was Jimmy Johnson and the Dallas Cowboys," Redskins defensive end Charles Mann said. "You start taking notice of his way of preparing these guys. These weren't Landry's Cowboys who would methodically beat you. These guys made big plays. Jimmy was a risk taker. I didn't get caught up in it, but there was definitely trash-talking. They were a different breed. It was definitely a different Dallas Cowboy team. Rough, kind of street [tough] with the bandannas. They were easier to hate."

Especially when they were winning titles you were used to winning yourself.

photo by Tracy Woodward/The Washington Times

Washington area native turned Cowboys running back Paul Palmer scores a touchdown, helping Dallas coach Jimmy Johnson record his first NFL victory.

Nov. 5, 1989

Meet The New Boss

Cowboys 13, Redskins 3

All was not well deep in the heart of Texas in 1989. Adopted Texan George Bush may have been in the White House, but the Lone Star State's favorite team was in deep trouble.

Arkansas oilman Jerry Jones had bought the Dallas Cowboys in 1989. In short order, Jones fired legendary coach Tom Landry and president Tex Schramm, the duo who had guided the Cowboys to 17 playoff berths and two Super Bowl titles in the previous 23 seasons but who hadn't won a playoff game in six years.

In place of Schramm and Landry went Jones — who hadn't been involved in football since starting on Arkansas' 1964 national champions — and Jimmy Johnson, his Razorbacks teammate. Johnson had been extraordinarily successful coaching in college, winning a national title at Miami, but he hadn't spent a day in the NFL and now he was taking over "America's Team."

"We had gone 3-1 in preseason, only losing late to Denver, and we were feeling pretty good," said Steve Walsh, then one of the Cowboys' rookie quarterbacks along with the injured Troy Aikman. "Jimmy thought he could win five or six games on his coaching ability alone. We had some good players, especially on offense. [Receiver] Michael Irvin, Mark Stepnoski, Kevin Gogan, Nate Newton, Mark Tuinei [all offensive linemen, who like Irvin would later go to Pro Bowls]. But Michael hadn't had a big rookie year, Step was a rookie, Kevin was a young guy, Mark hadn't made the transition to tackle [from defensive tackle] and Nate was just too heavy."

The Cowboys, coming off the 3-13 disaster of 1988, opened the season by getting blown out, 28-0, at New Orleans. After a 27-21 loss at Atlanta, host Dallas was crushed by Washington, 30-7.

The loss to the Redskins was the first of four straight by at least 17 points. Cowboys jokes were big in Dallas.

"We weren't even competitive," Walsh said. "Someone left a sign on my car at Texas Stadium that said, 'Would the woman who lost 11 children please report to the press box. They're beating the Cowboys 21-0.' They would bring in guys every Tuesday. We had 50-60 players in our team photo and only 35-40 were left by the end of the season."

The biggest personnel move Jones and Johnson made was a blockbuster. On October 12, they traded star running back Herschel Walker and three draft choices to Minnesota for five lesser players and eight picks, including first-rounders in 1990, 1991 and 1992. The deal rocked the NFL, but while it would fortify the Cowboys in the 1990s, it provided little immediate help.

After two closer defeats, 0-8 Dallas headed to Washington. Some players groused about Johnson's brutal practices, saying the longtime college coach didn't understand the pace of the NFL's 16-game season. Opposing defenses mocked the Cowboys' simple offense.

"We didn't have a lot of confidence, but we had a good gameplan and we were playing for [Dallas Hall of Famers] Roger Staubach, Bob Lilly and the rest of those guys," Walsh said. "Jimmy didn't exactly say that, but he did talk about the tradition before that game."

The usually-loquacious Johnson certainly couldn't say much about his Cowboys.

"I was hopeful we could be successful, but as bad as we were, I don't know that you could really say we had confidence going into the game," Johnson said. "We had a makeshift lineup with Paul Palmer at tailback [in Walker's place] and Steve [instead of top draft pick Aikman] at quarterback. But I knew our guys had a different spark about them practicing."

As safety Bill Bates — one of the few remaining links to the glory years — said, "We basically had nothing to lose."

While the Cowboys were just trying not to become the NFL's first 0-16 team with a matching second half of the season, the Redskins had their own problems. Less than two years removed from the Super Bowl XXII title, Washington was 4-4 and possibly headed to a second straight losing season. Cornerback Barry Wilburn would be suspended for a positive drug test the night of the Dallas game and Pro Bowl defensive end Dexter Manley would follow three weeks later

"It was a year of turmoil, a year of transition," said defensive end Charles Mann. "We were shuffling guys in and out on defense. We hadn't figured out who our quarterback was."

Mark Rypien had thrown three interceptions in a 37-24 loss to the Los Angeles Raiders the week before. That prompted Redskins coach Joe Gibbs to bench his young quarterback and replace him with Super Bowl XXII hero Doug Williams, who hadn't played in nearly 11 months and was just 10 weeks removed from back surgery.

"Of course I wanted to be in there, but I didn't think the move was unwarranted," said Rypien, who was second in the NFL with 14 touchdown passes but who had fumbled on all but one of the 12 times he had been sacked.

"Nothing was going right for us and Joe thought I might be the right medicine," said Williams, then 34.

"In retrospect, we kind of forced Doug back," said Washington general manager Charley Casserly. "We should have expected him to play the way he did."

So these were the Cowboys and Redskins who met on ESPN that night at RFK Stadium.

Washington had the ball first. Williams completed his first pass for 13 yards to receiver Art Monk. But running back Gerald Riggs was thrown for a loss and receiver Gary Clark dropped Williams' second throw, forcing a punt.

Dallas did nothing and Williams then led Washington 46 yards to the Dallas 27. However, two runs gained little and safety Vince Albritton then broke up a pass to Clark in the end zone. Chip Lohmiller hooked a 45-yard field goal try.

Now it was the Cowboys' turn to move. Walsh mixed short passes with handoffs to Palmer, who had starred at nearby Churchill High. When Palmer raced 20 yards down the left side, Dallas was at the Washington 16. But Walsh couldn't connect on two throws and kicker Roger Ruzek matched Lohmiller's miss with a 35-yard slice as the first quarter ended.

"When we were able to run the ball a little bit and we were playing good defense, I felt like we had a shot," Johnson said.

Despite Riggs and right guard Mark May joining an injury list which already included left tackle Jim Lachey and left guard Russ Grimm, Williams dissected Dallas's 26th-ranked defense with short passes before finding Monk for 22 yards. But on third-and-3 from the Dallas 25, blitzing safety Ray

Horton hit Williams. The pass wobbled into Albritton's arms.

"It's very disturbing when your quarterback's not where he should be," said Redskins defensive tackle Darryl Grant. "When the quarterback's off, it affects everybody. You get that 'oh-no' syndrome."

In the half's closing seconds, Williams failed to see Bates cutting in front of Clark and was picked off again.

"I'm not a guy who makes excuses, but it just wasn't me that night," said Williams, who was understandably troubled by the death of his beloved father just four days earlier.

Williams' numbers — 28-of-52 for 296 yards — were fine, but he couldn't produce a touchdown in what would be the penultimate start of his career.

"Sometimes I felt myself throwing off the wrong foot," Williams said. "I got hit one or two times. I never thought of coming out and I'm sure coach Gibbs didn't think that way either. It's not like I stunk up the joint. We all didn't play well."

Bates' interception – just the third of the year by a Cowboys defensive back – gave Dallas a first down on the Washington 34. On the subsequent third-and-4, Walsh made his best throw of the half on a 25-yard slant to Kelvin Martin. From the 2, Walsh missed Martin, but Ruzek's 20-yard field goal made it 3-0 Dallas at intermission as the RFK faithful booed.

"Joe and Richie [Petitbon, the defensive coordinator] maintained pretty good composure on the sideline, but in the locker room, they were pretty angry," Mann said. "Everybody was looking around like, 'What's happening? I don't know what's happening.' They were killing our defense. We were getting handled and it was a bad feeling. You didn't want to be their only win and you always hated to lose to the Cowboys."

The score may have been close, but the mood couldn't have been more different in the visitors' locker room.

"[Offensive coordinator] David Shula was so excited that we had a chance to win, he gave us his best pep talk," Walsh said.

However, it was the Redskins who bounced out of the locker room with renewed energy. The officials helped keep the eight-minute drive alive by ruling that Monk was down before he lost a fumble to cornerback Ron Francis. When halfback Jamie Morris was stopped on second-and-2 and Williams threw too low for receiver Ricky Sanders, Lohmiller's 35-yarder knotted the score at 3-3.

James Dixon returned the kickoff 39 yards to the Dallas 40. On third-and-3, Walsh fooled the Redskins, handing to Palmer out of the shotgun on a play the quarterback said, "was there all night." The 1986 Heisman Trophy runner-up had struggled in the NFL, but this time, he sprinted through a huge hole opened up by tackle Tuinei and guard Crawford Ker and raced 47 yards to the Washington 6. Two plays later, Palmer dived over from the 2 for the 10-3 lead.

"Palmer ran like an all-Pro back tonight," Bates said.

"We thought we could catch the Redskins off-balance since we were winless," Walsh said.

"They had a rag-team team so we walked in there thinking, 'These guys can't beat anybody,' but they were running the ball on us and racking up yards they shouldn't have," Grant said.

"They played better than us," said Washington offensive tackle Joe Jacoby, whose team would win five of its final six games to finish 10-6 but out of the playoffs on a tiebreaker. "We were flat and looked past them because of their record."

But that doesn't explain the previously winless Cowboys somehow not committing any turnovers or penalties.

"When you've got a team like we did, there's a tendency to think the other team was looking bad, but I don't think that was the case," said veteran Cowboys cornerback Everson Walls.

"You just don't come up here and beat the Redskins at RFK in a game they need," said Dallas defensive tackle Dean Hamel, who had been acquired from Washington in August.

"It's hard to believe you could be much lower than that," Casserly said.

"People were wondering whether this guy or that guy was washed-up," Grant remembered. "They were wondering what was wrong with the Redskins."

A lot in this game. They produced just two first downs on their next three series after Palmer's touchdown and when an unnecessary roughness penalty gave the Cowboys the ball on the Washington 44, Palmer scooted for six and then 14 of his career-high 110 yards to set up Ruzek's clinching 43-yard field goal with 4:03 to play.

"We didn't stop Palmer," Mann said. "He hit the holes fast. I'd be trying to shed

the block and he would be by me. Walsh didn't do much, but they were able to control the ball because Palmer kept busting out."

In contrast, Washington's league-leading offense was silenced by the defense of first-year Dallas coordinator Dave Wannstedt, managing a paltry 50 rushing yards on 21 carries.

"As the year went on, you could see the defense was getting better," Casserly said. "We hit them with some things in that first game that they weren't ready for, but after that, you could see why they became as good as they did. Wannstedt [who would become Chicago's coach four years later] knew what he was doing."

Walsh, who had starred for Johnson at Miami, ran over and gave the coach a hug and the ball as time ran out. Bates playfully mussed Johnson's helmet-like hair after just the Cowboys' second victory in 21 games (both against the Redskins).

"It was important for the team, for me and for Jimmy to get that first win," said Walsh, who was just 10-for-30 for 142 yards in his only victory as the Cowboys' starter. "It was a big relief to know that we weren't going to go 0-16. There were plenty of toasts and beer on the way home."

The Cowboys would play better the rest of the way but not win again to wind up 1-15.

"People knew we were rebuilding, and as long as we beat the Redskins that was fine." Johnson said.

But Jones was already thinking grander thoughts.

"We've got a long way to go, but I'll tell you, it's going to be awfully nice when we get there," Jones said as he celebrated his first NFL triumph.

Not even Jones knew how fast that prophecy would come true.

COWBOYS 13, REDSKINS 3

	1	2	3	4	TOTAL
COWBOYS	0	3	7	3	13
REDSKINS	0	0	3	0	3

◆ **SECOND QUARTER**
D - Ruzek 20 FG, D 3-0
W- Lohmiller 35 FG, 3-3

◆ **THIRD QUARTER**
D - Palmer 2 run (Ruzek kick), D 10-3

◆ **FOURTH QUARTER**
D - Ruzek 43 FG, D 13-3

Darrell Green

Washington Redskins cornerback Darrell Green refuses to say his semi-annual matchup with Dallas Cowboys receiver Michael Irvin is personal. No Muhammad Ali taunting Joe Frazier. It's more like two businessmen fighting for the same account.

"I could be on the ground fighting Michael Irvin, and we'll get up and go back to the huddle and I won't play him dirty the next play," Green said. "I'll play him the same the next play because we both have kept the concept that it's a team game. You don't see two players go off the field and fight. There is a rivalry within the game, but the game is still more important. You can't push and fight and play the game."

Green will likely break Monte Coleman's Redskins record of 216 career games late in the 1997 season. The six-time Pro Bowler said he's had plenty of tough matchups like Chicago Bears receiver Willie Gault, one of the few players who could press Green's speed.

But the Green-Irvin battles have been the measuring sticks of both perennial Pro Bowlers' careers. The winner of the matchup often gets the victory, too.

photo courtesy of the Washington Redskins

"It's a rivalry within a rivalry," said Redskins coach Norv Turner, the Cowboys' offensive coordinator from 1991-93. "You play someone twice a year for a number of years and both have been considered one of the best at their position. It's very competitive."

Physically, it would seem a mismatch. Irvin is 6-foot-3, 205 pounds. Green is 5-8, 184 pounds. The difference is Green won the NFL's fastest man competition three times following a college track career that included covering 100 meters in 10.08 seconds as a senior, second only to Olympic champion Carl Lewis.

"One of the reasons why the Redskins have had success against the Cowboys is Darrell has great quickness and has used it to combat Michael's size," Turner said. "Michael is able to shove and bang a little bit. Darrell has to play cat and mouse."

Said Irvin: "I know I'm not anywhere near as fast as Green is or anywhere as quick as he is so I use my size."

Green first saw the Redskins-Cowboys rivalry while growing up outside Houston. However, he admitted underestimating the series' intensity when arriving in Washington in 1983.

"What I saw as a kid is like a penny versus a million dollars," he said. "It's that big a contrast. When I walked into RFK, that was the rivalry. [Defensive coordinator Richie] Petitbon was telling me to stay calm, don't get too excited. I thought he was out of his mind. He said you haven't played the Dallas Cowboys at RFK. The fans were going crazy.

"We're talking about some of the big names from my childhood like Danny White and Drew Pearson. The only ones missing were Roger Staubach and Robert Newhouse. I was thinking about getting autographs, but Petitbon worked on me all week from getting autographs to getting mad and saying 'We've got to get these guys.'"

Green plans to remain in Washington after his career. He has started the Darrell Green Youth Life Foundation to provide educational opportunities for inner city children. However, he hasn't forgotten his roots.

"I'll fight for Washington, D.C.," Green said. "This is my home, but I'm a Texan as well. My friends back home tell me they're Cowboys fans, but they're still my friends, too."

Michael Irvin

Dallas Cowboys wide receiver Michael Irvin and Washington Redskins cornerback Darrell Green have been called "a rivalry within a rivalry." For one afternoon, it seemed a game within a game.

Entering the second 1991 meeting, Irvin led the NFC with 65 receptions while Green topped the NFL with five interceptions. The Cowboys decided to attack Green, a rare move against a fast corner with a penchant for pickoffs.

"I'm hoping to battle Darrell the good old fashion way, like two gladiators, one on one, mano a mano," Irvin said before the game. "That's what it's all about to face a challenge like that. I'll be competing against the best corner in the NFL."

Irvin caught nine passes for 131 yards and one touchdown over Green in the Cowboys' 24-21 victory. Seven catches were for first downs or a touchdown.

"I should have played better," Irvin deadpanned. "I dropped a couple."

Said Cowboys quarterback Troy Aikman: "We always felt going in that was an important matchup for us to win, and we felt we could. Michael had some big games against Darrell, and we were able to make some plays with Michael."

Redskins coach Norv Turner was the Cowboys offensive coordinator for that 1991 matchup. He admits to purposely picking on Green even though the Redskins corner was enjoying what would be his fifth Pro Bowl season.

"People first recognized Michael as one of the great receivers from that 1991 game," Turner said. "Michael made a bunch of catches and stepped up a level in the way experts perceived him."

photo courtesy of the Dallas Cowboys

Green has five interceptions against the Cowboys and has twice limited Irvin to one catch during the nine-year biannual matchup. But Green admits Irvin, a six-time Pro Bowler, got the better of him that day.

"This was a game I couldn't have written my name properly," Green said. "They just got me. It very easily could have gone the other way. There was only one route where he totally beat me. All I had to do was intercept one and Norv would have said 'Let's call this instead.' "

Even Irvin admits he was surprised Dallas tested Green so much that afternoon.

"Nobody throws at Darrell, and it's not a dumb move," he said. "You get that impression because it's a known fact."

Irvin has caught 76 passes and nine touchdowns in 15 games against Washington so he's often successful against the Redskins. Green concedes that 1991 meeting, but not the career matchup, saying, "A guy like that averaging five a game isn't bad. He caught five against the Washington Redskins, not Darrell Green."

photo by Ross Franklin/The Washington Times

Dallas receiver Alvin Harper outleaps the Washington defense for a crushing score just before halftime in 1991.

Nov. 24, 1991

How 'Bout Them Cowboys

Cowboys 24, Redskins 21

Neither team will ever know what might have been, if this one game simultaneously prevented and created NFL history on a rather unsuspecting Sunday afternoon in RFK Stadium.

After all, there were few clues of extenuating ramifications. The Washington Redskins were 11-0 and just had polished off their past two opponents by a combined 97-31. They had totaled 1,021 yards, 816 passing yards and nine touchdown passes. Plus, the Redskins already had beaten the Cowboys once this year, 33-31, and had won 15 of their past 16 games, not to mention 11 straight at RFK.

No wonder the Redskins were 13-point favorites coming in, these NFL somebodies rolling toward the league's first undefeated, 16-game season.

"The hoopla was about us going undefeated," said Washington defensive end Charles Mann. "That got bigger than the game. It was almost like the Cowboys were an afterthought."

Quite understandable. The Cowboys were NFL nobodies, merely 6-5, and without a winning season since 1985. They had just lost their past two games, and three of four. This would be their third consecutive road game, a Herculean stretch for a team just 27 games removed from a 1-15 season.

"We had not done anything yet to show we could be an above average football team," Cowboys quarterback Troy Aikman says.

Maybe that is why Dallas coach Jimmy Johnson played a hunch in this 12th game of the 1991 season as aggressively as he is known to play blackjack. The Cowboys were coming off a 22-9 loss to the New York Giants and 26-23 overtime loss to Houston. A third consecutive loss and a matchup with Pittsburgh just four days away could have sent Dallas spiraling toward its sixth consecutive losing season.

"Everything was stacked against us, and I had to do something to at least give our guys the thought we had a chance to win the ballgame," Johnson said. "If I approached it as a normal game, in the back of their minds, they would have said, 'Hey, we're not good enough to beat them.'

"So I just kind of said to myself I'm going to throw caution to the wind, and what the hell, what did we have to lose?"

Johnson wasn't totally irrational, though. He knew the Cowboys nearly had beaten Washington in Week 2, having taken an early 21-10 lead, only to see running back Emmitt Smith become so sick to his stomach from drinking Carboplex — a carbohydrate supplement — that he could carry the ball only twice for three yards the second half after a 109-yard first half. Plus, Aikman and wide receiver Michael Irvin were on their way to their first Pro Bowl; and Smith was on his way toward becoming the first Cowboys running back to win an NFL rushing title.

So Johnson began hatching his plot, working on an on-side kick and fake kicks; intimating fourth downs would not be conventional and Hail Mary's more than a Sunday prayer.

"We changed all our tendencies because teams that had played them close to the vest prior to that had gotten beaten," Johnson said. "The Redskins were too good that year."

Johnson also concocted a theme.

"I think Teddy Roosevelt said, 'Don't ever hit a man lightly, always carry a big stick,' " Johnson said. "And so I just came up with an analogy. I actually pulled out [guard] John Gesek, and said, 'If I'm going to hit a big ol' gorilla, I'm not going to tap him lightly.' And I said, 'John come up here,' and this was in practice, and I said, 'Now if I'm going to hit John, obviously I'm not going to tap him lightly. If I'm going to hit him, I'm going to hit him with everything I've got.'

"Everybody laughed and I said, 'And then I'd probably run like hell after I hit him.'

"So I said, 'But what I'm trying to tell you is we're not going to go in there and play it close to the vest. We're going to pull out all the stops, and with everything we've got. Get them to thinking this team came here to win.' "

Johnson had hit a chord.

"We had confidence going into the game because, whether it's true or not, Jimmy had concocted the image that after studying film and game planning, if he called these things during the game in certain situations they would work," said Cowboys snapper Dale Hellestrae.

Maybe the team gleaned some confidence from the gorilla theory, but Cowboys owner Jerry Jones saw how uneasy his coach felt before the game.

"He was down," Jones said. "He was very pessimistic. Dave [Wannstedt, defensive coordinator] was having to prop him up. I remember Jimmy saying, 'I hope we get out of here without being so deflated so we can continue to compete this year.'"

If Johnson was playing with scared money he did not show it. Early he allowed kicker Ken Willis to attempt a 51-yard field goal that was deflected short. Trailing 7-0 after cornerback Martin Mayhew's 31-yard interception return for a touchdown, Johnson ordered his first fourth-down gamble, Aikman hooking up with Irvin for six yards on fourth-and-5. Three plays later, on third-and-15 from the 32, offensive coordinator Norv Turner had the temerity to call a draw.

"If we caught them in the right defense, it had the potential of being a big gainer," Smith said of the draw. "And what happened was we lined up, and they were in a defense we practiced against all week. Well, I knew we could get positive yards out of it. Once I got the ball and got to the line of scrimmage, I knew I had an opportunity to turn the corner.

"And once I turned the corner, it was over with."

Smith might have tied the score, but Johnson clutched his big stick even tighter, calling for the onside kick. And even though the Cowboys recovered, but did nothing with the possession, Johnson had definitely set the tempo.

"When we went for the onside kick and recovered it, that got everybody excited," Aikman said. "It was like, hey, he said we were going to do it, we knew we were going to do it and it worked."

The Redskins had to be growing uneasy. Already there had been a 51-yard field goal attempt, two fourth-down attempts, a draw on third-and-15 and an onside kick. What in the world would be next?

A Hail Mary?

Even that was rather unconventional. Sure Dallas was out of timeouts, facing a fourth-and-7 at the Washington 34 with the game still tied. But there were 13 seconds left in the half, one in which the Redskins had totaled only 83 total yards. A field goal would have been huge. So would have a first down. Plus, these Hail Mary attempts for the Cowboys had been more like an Act of Contrition: Aikman already had been intercepted six times on these desperation heaves. He had yet to complete one.

Aikman lined up three receivers right: Kelvin Martin inside, Irvin outside and Harper in the middle.

"I was supposed to be the first one to get to the end zone," Harper said. "I was supposed to act like a setter in volleyball. If I could catch the ball, great, but if I couldn't I was supposed to tip it and keep it alive."

When Harper arrived in the end zone, there was a cluster of Redskins, but Harper, at 6-foot-4, was a good four inches taller than the nearest Redskins defender, and had plenty of room to post up.

"Troy had just said, 'Let's go down, throw it up and hope someone can make a play on it,'" Harper said. "I told the guys in the huddle to get ready to congratulate me in the end zone. And when I got there, no one was really around me. [Safety] Brad Edwards was behind me, but there was no one in front of me. I saw the ball coming and thought, 'It's mine.'"

It was nearly as if Harper had called for the ball, causing everyone else to scatter. Aikman might have been the most stunned when Harper made the catch and the Cowboys took a 14-7 lead into the locker room.

"It's the only one I remember working," Aikman said.

Johnson immediately grabbed him on the sideline and said, "I think the worm is turning."

Well, if the worm was turning, it didn't quite make 180 degrees. Five plays into the third quarter as Aikman released a pass that would go to Martin for 27 yards and a first down at the Washington 37, Redskins defensive tackle Jumpy Geathers and Mann scissor-tackled the quarterback, spraining his right knee. Aikman was helped off the field. He was through for the regular season.

Enter backup Steve Beuerlein, acquired in a trade with the Los Angeles Raiders just before the season began.

"Sure it was a big concern," Johnson said of losing Aikman. "Beuerlein showed in that game that he plays better than he practices. In practice, you really can't compare 95 percent of the quarterbacks around to Troy's accuracy. So Beuerlein never really looked good in practice because we were comparing him to Troy."

Not diverging one iota from his swashbuckling ways, Turner ordered a bomb for Harper on Beuerlein's first play.

"He stepped in with a pool of confidence," Smith said of Beuerlein, who was playing his first consequential plays for Dallas. "He stepped in and said, 'Don't worry about it. Don't worry about Troy, there is nothing we can do about it. Just make plays, and everything will take care of itself.' That was his attitude."

Beuerlein's first pass would have been right on

the money. But when Mayhew grasped for Harper in desperation at the 17, he was flagged for a 20-yard interference penalty. No matter that Willis missed a 32-yard field goal try, the tone was maintained.

"With Michael being our best receiver – our go-to-guy – if we've ever gone into a game and felt we are not going to be able to get the ball to Michael, that was a big concern," Aikman said.

So the Monday before the game Turner told Irvin, "We're going to run our offense no matter who's playing who."

Or who's throwing to you, for that matter.

Irvin already had caught five passes for 66 yards in the first half. He already had converted one fourth-down attempt and his 16-yard reception was the impetus for the Hail Mary. And if not for a false start, Irvin would have been credited with a 48-yard reception to the Washington 4 late in the third quarter.

No matter, though, because on the next play Beuerlein threw to Irvin for 17, and four plays later, just seconds into the fourth quarter, Beuerlein again went to Irvin on a second-and-7 at the Washington 23. The Redskins blitzed. Beuerlein fired to Irvin, smothered by Green. But the Cowboys' wideout turned "Playmaker," juggled the ball twice before disappearing from Green for the touchdown and a 21-7 lead.

"This was a game where I couldn't have written my name properly," Green said of Irvin's nine catches for 130 yards against him. "They just got me. It very easily could have gone the other way. All I had to do was intercept one [pass], and Norv would have said, 'Let's call this instead.' "

But Green wasn't the Redskins' only problem. With 11:48 left to play Washington had totaled just 155 yards. Quarterback Mark Rypien had completed just three passes to The Posse: receivers Art Monk, Gary Clark and Ricky Sanders. And Rypien responded to the Cowboys' latest touchdown by throwing an interception on the first play, cornerback Larry Brown picking off the deep ball intended for Clark.

The Redskins would mount a mild fourth-quarter protest, scoring two touchdowns to one Willis field goal, but they never came within seven points until the final 18 seconds.

So there would be no undefeated season, NFL history preserved. Further galling the Redskins must have been losing just once more that year, dropping a 24-22 decision to Phila-

delphia in the final game after Gibbs decided to rest the majority of his starters in the second half with a 19-7 lead.

If only the Redskins had beaten the Cowboys …

"I don't think it was a question of letting down or losing focus," Rypien said. "The Cowboys just outplayed us that day. You would like to think [the unbeaten streak] could go on forever, but you're going to lose. You just hate to lose to that team, especially in your stadium."

The Cowboys weren't so choosy. At that point in 1991 they just wanted to beat someone good. And the victory, despite the loss of Aikman, rocketed the Cowboys into a season-ending five-game winning streak, allowing them to finish with a winning record [11-5] for the first time since 1985. The victory also propelled the Cowboys toward their first playoff appearance since 1985 and first playoff victory since 1982.

And maybe, just maybe, the victory over the Redskins, soon to be Super Bowl champs, gave the Cowboys enough confidence and enough momentum to eventually become *The Cowboys* once again, winning back-to-back Super Bowl titles in 1992-93 and again in 1995. Maybe just as crucial, as far as long-standing Dallas fans were concerned, was wrestling NFC East dominance away from Washington for the next five years.

"There's no question [the victory] got coach Johnson and that group of Cowboys headed in the right direction – toward winning back-to-back Super Bowls," Turner said. "You go beat a team that's headed to the Super Bowl, and beat them in their own place in a game that wasn't close, well, that was the turning point for that group."

Leaving only historians to wonder what if the struggling Cowboys had not beaten the undefeated Redskins, 24-21, Nov. 24, 1991, at RFK Stadium?

COWBOYS 24, REDSKINS 21

	1	2	3	4	TOTAL
COWBOYS	0	14	0	10	24
REDSKINS	7	0	0	14	21

◆ **FIRST QUARTER**
W - Mayhew 31 interception return (Lohmiller kick), W 7-0

◆ **SECOND QUARTER**
D - E. Smith 32 run (Willis kick), 7-7
D - Harper 34 pass from Aikman (Willis kick), D 14-7

◆ **FOURTH QUARTER**
D - Irvin 23 pass from Beuerlein (Willis kick), D 21-7
W - Riggs 1 run (Lohmiller kick), D 21-14
D - Willis 42 FG, D 24-14
W - Sanders 29 pass from Rypien (Lohmiller kick), D 24-21

photo by Kevin Gilbert/The Washington Times

Dallas defensive tackle Leon Lett shows Washington quarterback Mark Rypien who's boss in the 1992 opener.

Sept. 7, 1992

Talkin' The Talk

Cowboys 23, Redskins 10

They needled the Redskins all game, predicting stardom for themselves and an end to Washington's reign.

Not that the Redskins heard every word. With a jacked-up crowd roaring every minute, waves of sound crashed into their ears, preventing them from hearing much of anything else, including audibles.

Dallas longed for this moment, having waited nearly a decade for a return to prominence. The Cowboys, and their fans, were intent on enjoying this night. And, in this new regime, personalities weren't constricted.

That changed when Jimmy Johnson replaced Tom Landry as coach. Out went muzzled players; in came outward displays of confidence. Johnson's Cowboys were young and talented and they knew it.

In his three seasons, Dallas' record shot from 1-15 to 11-5. As 1992 started, the Cowboys demanded attention from the top teams. So it was time for them to let the world know — not that they hadn't already.

"We breathed a little sigh of relief about not having to face them in the [1991 NFC] Championship Game," said Washington quarterback Mark Rypien. "You knew the Cowboys were an up-and-coming team."

They just didn't have to like it. The Redskins were an older team, one that had dominated the previous season en route to a Super Bowl title. Washington entered this game, and season, wanting to prove the championship was no fluke.

In 1991, eight Redskins made the Pro Bowl; Rypien was remarkable; the offensive line allowed just nine sacks; the defensive line stuffed the run. It's no wonder Washington had won 17 of 19 games. And those two losses — including a 24-21 defeat to Dallas which dropped the Redskins to 11-1 — came by a combined five points.

On the flip side, Dallas, absent from the Super Bowl since 1978, ached for such success. It showed. The Cowboys pointed to this opener as a chance to make their first large statement. And making statements seemed to be something they enjoyed.

The Cowboys' core was a bunch of twentysomethings prone to exuberance, led by receivers Michael Irvin and Alvin Harper. That clashed with the Redskins' just-do-your job mentality.

"It was definitely a different Dallas team," Redskins end Charles Mann said. "They were easier to hate."

But the cue of confidence permeated from Johnson, whose University of Miami teams had exhibited similar traits.

Here's confidence: Because of their offseason preparations for Washington, Johnson said he told his assistants, "We'll take care of the Redskins. We just have to make sure we're ready for the [New York] Giants the next week."

That attitude trickled down to the players, still smarting from the previous season's playoff loss to Detroit. The Cowboys were thinking big.

"If we could win the [NFC] East then we felt we could go on and win the Super Bowl," said Dallas quarterback Troy Aikman. "The Redskins were the big bullies, the guys we had to unseat. Going into that particular game, there wasn't any doubt we could compete with them or beat them — we had done that every year we had been here — but we knew we would have to play well because we had tremendous respect for them."

Johnson and his staff felt good despite the holdouts of Irvin, tight end Jay Novacek and center Mark Stepnoski. Novacek signed one week before the game while Irvin, after some anxious moments, signed on Sept. 3. Neither got much work in with the team. Stepnoski signed two days before and didn't play versus Washington.

Irvin, though his agent wondered only days earlier if he'd get signed, said he never doubted he'd play against the Redskins.

"Hell, no," Irvin said. "Are you crazy? Do you think I'd miss all that fun?"

To make sure it was a fun night — and season — Aikman faxed Irvin and Novacek pages of the playbook during training camp. Aikman also sent any notes he had made about a particular play or read.

"At least when they came in they had heard some

of the things that I sent," Aikman said. "[But] we pulled back on some of the things we were doing and did things those guys were comfortable doing the year before. Michael still had a big game."

But Washington had its share of holdouts, too. Rypien, offensive tackle Jim Lachey and cornerback Darrell Green — Pro Bowlers in 1991 — all had contract problems, as did first-round pick Desmond Howard.

Though all eventually reported to training camp — Lachey, Green and Howard appeared in one preseason game; Rypien in two — the Redskins weren't crisp.

"When you have all five linemen in camp and working together, you have a feeling that you're going to have a good year," said Lachey, who remained in Columbus, Ohio. "When one's missing, it makes it tough on the whole group.

"It's a tough thing [holding out]. I could never hold out in the city I play in. I don't want to hear about it on the radio or see it on TV. You want to be out there. On the other hand, you know you can't play forever and you have to get what you can while the value is there."

It didn't help Lachey that he had to face pass-rushing end Charles Haley, acquired by Dallas from San Francisco in a trade two days before the final preseason game. Haley's presence offset the injuries to starting defensive tackles Tony Casillas and Russell Maryland. The Cowboys even started a rookie — middle linebacker Robert Jones.

Dallas also had something else unexpected on its side: A raucous crowd, spirited perhaps by the sale of alcohol in Texas Stadium for the first time. To the Redskins, that noise proved damaging.

They entered Texas Stadium with a game plan that had worked in the previous Super Bowl. Run the no-huddle and bark out plays at the line.

"I thought we had one of the best game plans we ever had for the Cowboys," said Redskins' coach Joe Gibbs. "Noise had never been a problem at Texas Stadium. It turns out that was one of my worst coaching jobs."

The first series showed why. The line and backs missed Rypien's audible on the first play and linebacker Vinson Smith sprinted in untouched to sack Rypien for an 11-yard loss to the 9. On second down, running back Earnest Byner was nailed for a 3-yard loss and on third down, Haley pressured Rypien into a bad throw.

"You're standing next to Ryp and you can't hear a thing he's saying," Lachey said. "I told Ryp, 'Look my way when you say the count so I can hear you.' He said, 'What about the right tackle?' I said, 'Hey, I've got Haley over here. Who do you want to get hit by?'"

Then, on fourth down, John Brandes' high snap to punter Kelly Goodburn resulted in a blocked kick by Issiac Holt and a safety.

"That was the key play in the game," Johnson said. "That set the stage."

The world was the Cowboys' stage this night. Dallas' first possession showed its strength and diversity. The Cowboys marched 84 yards in 13 plays and took a 9-0 lead when Smith scored from the 5. On the drive, Aikman completed 4-of-6 passes for 41 yards and Smith carried seven times for 28 yards. A 15-yard personal foul on Washington safety Brad Edwards contributed as well.

Stopping Smith proved to be troublesome, as it had the previous three meetings. In 1991, only one running back gained more than 100 yards against the Redskins. It was Smith, who did it twice.

He had no problem on this night, either. This would be his fourth straight game with more than 100 yards versus Washington. No running back had accomplished such a feat against the Redskins under Gibbs.

"You would stop him, stop him, stop him," Mann said. "But you knew that sooner or later, Emmitt was going to bust one. At halftime, we would say, 'All right. We've got him under control.' And then we would see he already had 71 yards. I respect that guy so much."

Aikman said, "Maybe, as much as anything, we always knew we were going to have tough games against them and the offensive line got pretty geared up and Emmitt got geared up and we were able to have success."

Smith gained 79 yards in the first half of this game, but it was the passing attack that accounted for Dallas' second touchdown. It came two series after Washington had cut the lead to 9-7. Cornerback Martin Mayhew's interception had led to a three-play, 58-yard drive that ended with Rypien's 30-yard scoring toss to receiver Gary Clark.

Then, with 1:37 remaining in the first half, Aikman went to work. He needed only 35 seconds to complete a six-play, 67-yard drive.

Dallas thought touchdown the whole way. On third-and-10 from the Washington 26, rather than getting conservative, offensive co-ordinator Norv Turner called for a lob to receiver Alvin Harper. Aikman's pass was perfect and the 6-foot-4 Harper beat 5-8 cornerback Darrell Green for the score.

"To this day, Darrell says I pushed, but I didn't," Harper said.

Dallas, though, was pushing Washington around. The first-half statistics proved that as the Cowboys had outgained the Redskins 279-111 — including 112 to minus-2 in the first quarter.

But Dallas' offense didn't need to do anything for its only second-half score. With just under seven minutes remaining in the third quarter, Goodburn punted to Kelvin Martin, who fielded the ball at the 21.

Four Redskins surrounded Martin. Somehow, he escaped by cutting to his left and, thanks to three clearing blocks, raced up the sideline for the score and a 23-7 lead. Special teams, once a Washington staple, had become a trouble spot.

Still, a stunned Washington recovered on its next drive. The Redskins moved from their own 18 to the Cowboys' 23 in 13 plays. But this was not Washington's night and the drive fell apart. A first down pass interference penalty on Clark pushed the ball back to the 33. On third down, Lachey, bracing for Haley, moved early and suddenly it was third-and-19. Byner gained one yard and Chip Lohmiller followed with a 49-yard field goal with 1:22 elapsed in the final quarter.

The Redskins' next possession ended with three Rypien incompletions — the final one into the end zone — from the Dallas 28. The Cowboys chewed up the final 5:51.

Dallas showed its mettle as its star players commanded the spotlight. Irvin, despite missing nearly the entire camp, still caught five passes for 89 yards. Smith rushed for 139 yards on 26 carries. Aikman was efficient at the right times, completing 18-of-31 passes for 216 yards, one touchdown and one interception. But he was a combined 6-for-8 for 91 yards and a touchdown in the final meaningful drive of each half.

Haley, whom the 49ers seemed pleased to deal, had one sack and harassed Rypien all night. Haley's addition solidified the defense and paved the way for a Super Bowl victory at the end of this season. Not bad for a guy who had undergone rotator cuff surgery in March and arthroscopic knee surgery three weeks before the game.

"The thing we had to have that we didn't have in '91 was pass defense," Johnson said. "And pass defense is a pass rush and coverage. We added the coverage through the draft [with cornerback Kevin Smith in the first round and safety Darren Woodson in the second] and added the rush through the trade for Charles Haley. He pressured them."

And the league. Haley proved to be the final ingredient Dallas needed to win a Super Bowl as the Cowboys first ripped through the league, finishing 13-3, and then Buffalo. They crushed the Bills, 52-17, in Super Bowl XXVII in Pasadena.

While the Redskins gained revenge in the second meeting that season — beating the Cowboys 20-17 on safety Danny Copeland's end-zone fumble recovery — their days on top had ended.

Washington overcame devastating injuries and reached the playoffs at 9-7, nearly upsetting San Francisco in the second round. Within three months, Gibbs would retire.

Time had run out and the Cowboys were eager to show the Redskins the door.

"They were look at us as a team on the way down and they were rubbing it in," Washington's right tackle Joe Jacoby said of that season-opening defeat.

But what could the Redskins do?

"They were saying, 'You might be the world champs, but it's our turn now,' " Lachey said. "You get tired of hearing that. You could show them your ring after the game, but it doesn't mean anything when they beat you."

COWBOYS 23, REDSKINS 10

	1	2	3	4	TOTAL
REDSKINS	0	7	0	3	10
COWBOYS	9	7	7	0	23

◆ **FIRST QUARTER**
D - Punt blocked out of end zone for safety, D 2-0
D - Smith 5 run (Elliott kick), D 9-0

◆ **SECOND QUARTER**
W - Clark 30 pass from Rypien (Lohmiller kick), D 9-7
D - Harper 26 pass from Aikman (Elliott kick), D 16-7

◆ **THIRD QUARTER**
D - Martin 79 punt return (Elliott kick), D 23-7

◆ **FOURTH QUARTER**
W - Lohmiller 49 FG, D 23-10

Norv Turner

Dallas quarterbacks have never been favorites of Washington coaches. But before coach Norv Turner came to Washington, no Redskin had ever coached a Cowboys quarterback.

Cowboys quarterback Troy Aikman and Turner have remained close since the latter departed Dallas for Washington in 1994. They talk regularly on the phone and see each other in the offseason. Turner knows Washington fans think Redskins coaches should hate their rivals, but that would be betraying his old friends, particularly Aikman.

"I don't see it as a conflict with football at all," said Turner, the Cowboys' offensive coordinator from 1991-93. "From a competitive standpoint, there's no question this rivalry is greater than anyone involved. Because of the rivalry, the distance between the cities and our hectic schedules, I have probably seen Troy once in each of the offseasons, but we still communicate. Most of it is dealing with our family. He's close to my children and my wife."

Still, having a Cowboy become a Redskins coach was like pulling the Trojan horse inside the fortress walls. Washington fans want Dallas haters like coach George Allen, who once offered to fight Cowboys coach Tom Landry at midfield for the game's outcome and fined any player who called defensive end Dallas Hickman by his first name.

But Turner's background prevents him from

photo courtesy of the Washington Redskins

disliking Dallas. During Turner's three seasons with the Cowboys, Dallas went 43-13 while winning consecutive Super Bowls in 1992-93. Turner sometimes said "we" when referring to the Cowboys during his opening days in Washington, but it soon stopped.

"I don't think it took me long to become comfortable with Washington," Turner said. "Maybe it took people awhile to get comfortable with me. Once you move a couple times [during your career] you know you're committed to making that team the best it can be."

The Redskins have steadily rebuilt under Turner, going 3-13, 6-10 and 9-7. Turner is 3-3 against Dallas, including a sweep in 1995. Turner realizes the rivalry makes for strange encounters.

"People ask me how can your team get up to beat Dallas [and not anyone else] and would ask [former Cowboys coach] Jimmy Johnson how can they be 1-15 and the one win be against the Redskins?" Turner said. "This is a game where the players and fans take over no matter who the coaches are."

But Turner is still beloved in Dallas as part of the Cowboys return to the NFL's elite.

"It's still amazing three years later when I go through an airport," he said, "and people come up to me and introduce themselves as big Dallas Cowboys fans and thank me for what I did down there."

Troy Aikman

When Dallas offensive coordinator Norv Turner left to become the Washington coach, Cowboys quarterback Troy Aikman joked about taking a collection from players to retain his mentor.

"Norv and my relationship was pretty unique," Aikman said. "I don't know that I will have that type of relationship with a coach again. I hadn't up to that point, and I haven't since. I think of him as almost like a brother."

Turner was an up-and-coming head coaching prospect from the Los Angeles Rams who would become the Cowboys' offensive coordinator for three seasons (1991-93) and two Super Bowl championships. Aikman was Dallas' first rookie starting quarterback since Roger Staubach (1969), and struggled during his first two seasons with a 7-19 record. Neither Turner nor Aikman were quite sure of the other's potential, but within three years formed one of the strongest coach-player relationships in the NFL.

"Troy and I hit it right off," Turner said. "As an assistant coach with quarterbacks, you spend so much time with each other that you either really like each other or dislike each other. There's not much middle ground there. We have similar likes and dislikes, we both value similar things in people and it was easy to communicate and get along. I was able to help him progress and he was able to help me progress."

Said Aikman: "We shared some really beautiful times, but then there was some tough times as well. I think we were able to help each other through difficult periods."

Aikman felt a kinship with Turner because both were trying to move to a higher level. Aikman wanted to be a Pro Bowl starter while Turner was elevated from an assistant coach to an offensive coordinator.

"It was a big step for him to make from a wide receivers coach to running an offense and wanting to do well," Aikman said. "There were some doubts in his mind as to how well he was going to do."

Together, Turner and Aikman took an offense that included running back Emmitt Smith, tight end Jay Novacek and receiver Michael Irvin to Super Bowl championships in 1992-93 before Turner departed for Washington. Aikman again led Dallas to the title in 1995.

As a Rams assistant, Turner helped mold quarterback Jim Everett into a Pro Bowl passer. Now it was Aikman's turn. Aikman reached the Pro Bowl in his first year with Turner, and has since made six straight. He's now 80-24 as a starter, 10-2 in the post-season, and ranks first among Cowboys quarterbacks in career passing yards and completions.

Aikman is 3-1 against the Redskins since Turner left, but neither believes he has an edge versus the other after working so closely together. Aikman admitted he roots for Turner to do well in Washington as long as it doesn't come at Dallas' expense.

"I found myself really wanting him to do well, for the Redskins to do well," Aikman said. "But now, Washington has kind of turned the corner and has been extremely competitive."

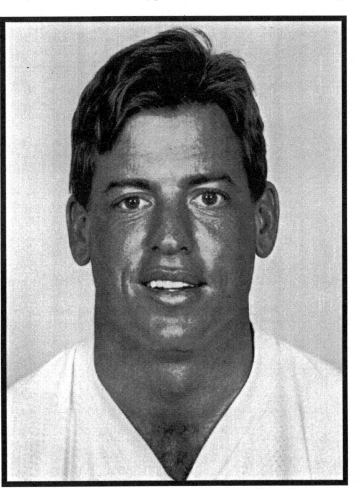

photo courtesy of the Dallas Cowboys

photo by Arnie Sachs/Consolidated News Pictures
Two men who replaced coaching legends, Washington's Richie Petitbon and Dallas' Jimmy Johnson, share a moment before 1993's first game.

Sept. 6, 1993

Opening Statement
Redskins 35, Cowboys 16

Joe Gibbs wasn't there, absent from the Washington sideline for the first time since 1980. That should have caused concern. But it didn't. Richie Petitbon, Gibbs' trusted defensive coordinator, was in charge. And his presence righted those left staggering by Gibbs' retirement.

Especially the players.

"The big thing was, we were still the Redskins," said offensive lineman Raleigh McKenzie. "We were still the guys who had won the championship [two years] before."

Dallas' All-Pro running back Emmitt Smith stayed home, too. But he wasn't ready for retirement. Just a hefty raise. And his understudy, untested rookie Derrick Lassic, failed to calm rising fears. Not the Cowboys or their fans. This transition tested their patience.

Turns out the season opener only heightened each side's feelings. Petitbon's coaching wasn't the only reason behind Washington's 35-16 Monday Night home victory. Nor was Lassic to blame in defeat. After all, he did gain 75 yards on 16 carries.

But after this game, Washington was stoked as talk centered around a return to the Super Bowl. Minus Gibbs.

In Dallas, fear mounted as the sign-Emmitt-now campaign escalated. Without him, a successful Super Bowl defense was unlikely. The organization knew it.

"We were in disarray because *our guy* wasn't there," said Dallas coach Jimmy Johnson. "And that was 90 percent of the focus of our football team. Even though I said we were fine and that we could play without him, I had it in the back of my mind that he would show, right on up to Wednesday before the game. I know we weren't as prepared to play as we should have been mentally, and even technically, not having him."

Or, put simply, Dallas offensive tackle Mark Tuinei said, "We thought we needed Emmitt because we did."

Tuinei wasn't alone.

"The coaches kept telling us, 'Hey [Lassic is] good. We won't miss Emmitt that much,'" said snapper Dale Hellestrae. "And the players were going, 'Yeah right.'

"And [Washington was] gunned up."

For two reasons. First was the Redskins' 1992 season, one that finished with a 9-7 regular season record and a 20-13 second-round loss at San Francisco in the playoffs.

Quarterback Mark Rypien's day typified the Redskins' year. In 1991, he was named the MVP of the Super Bowl. But in the next season his costly fumble late in the fourth quarter ended a drive deep in 49ers' territory.

Then there was Petitbon. Few understood the Washington-Dallas rivalry better than Petitbon. He arrived in 1971 — when this two-city feud was about to explode — via the Los Angeles Rams.

Petitbon started at safety for two seasons and played on the Redskins' first NFC Championship team. Six years later coach Jack Pardee hired him as an assistant. Three years later, Gibbs appointed Petitbon defensive coordinator.

Theirs was a marriage of opposites. Gibbs, a born-again Christian, believed in hard work. Even if it took all night, which it often did. On those occasions, he slept on a cot in his office. Petitbon, a former partying member of the famed Over the Hill Gang, got his work done. Then bolted. Even if it was early evening.

Gibbs liked conservative attacks. Petitbon preferred gambling schemes.

But both styles worked. And both earned the praise of their players for halftime adjustments, particularly in that Super Bowl season of 1991.

"He never second-guessed me," Petitbon said of Gibbs. "There was no friction at all."

Others noticed his input and wooed Petitbon. But, at various times, he turned down Indianapolis, Tampa Bay, New England and Denver. Chicago (where he played) and New Orleans (where he was born), among others, considered him a finalist for head coaching vacancies. Those jobs went to Dave Wannstedt and Jim Mora, respectively, and Petitbon remained a Redskin.

Then, on March 5, 1993, Gibbs stunned

Washington with his decision to retire after 12 seasons. The organization immediately named Petitbon as his successor.

"To see this job go to someone else would have been a disaster," said Petitbon, the only member of the organization to have played or coached in every Redskins' Super Bowl appearance. "[But] let's face it. Time was running out for me."

His players were thrilled and carried that excitement into the season opener.

"If you ever wanted something real badly, it was that opening game against Dallas," said Washington defensive end Charles Mann. "We didn't want it for ourselves so much. We wanted it for Richie. This was an opportunity for us to affirm the signing of Richie Petitbon as our coach, a player's coach, a good guy. We wanted to show the world that the Redskins were still there. How do we show it? By going out there and thrashing the Cowboys. Everybody was extremely focused. We just systematically whipped their behinds. We went crazy in the locker room. We knocked them off their high horse. People say they didn't have Emmitt. We knew there was going to be a blemish on that win. We didn't want any blemishes for Richie."

Besides, Washington was missing one of its top players, offensive tackle Jim Lachey. In the exhibition opener against Cleveland, he had torn the anterior cruciate ligament in his right knee and was lost for the season. Mo Elewonibi replaced Lachey, a Pro Bowler in 1990 and 1991.

And the popular line heard in Washington after this game: Emmitt doesn't play defense. End Charles Haley, linebacker Ken Norton, tackle Russell Maryland and safety Darren Woodson did. And that's where Dallas faltered on this night.

But Smith, watching the game with his family, said he could have changed the outcome. Or, at least, had an impact.

"Yeah, I would have made a difference," said Smith, who had rushed for 1,713 yards and 18 touchdowns the previous season. "I was sick, man, having to sit there and watch it. It was too hard to sit there and watch it. That sucked ... That really sucked. I was cheering on the ballclub as if I was there. And mad because I wasn't there. I thought they were going to win too."

His confidence stemmed from the game's early signs. First, Washington's Chip Lohmiller missed a 32-yard field goal attempt, which was set up when Pat Eilers recovered a fumbled punt.

Four plays later, quarterback Troy Aikman's 80-

yard touchdown pass to receiver Alvin Harper on a post-pattern gave Dallas the early lead. The Cowboys capitalized on a miscommunication between cornerback AJ Johnson and safety Danny Copeland. Harper, the third option on the play, scored easily.

But the Cowboys' cheering soon stopped. Lin Elliott missed the extra point and Washington seized control. The Redskins did it on the ground, just as they used to under Gibbs.

They had planned to do it differently, however. Gibbs had used a one-back, two tight-end scheme. New offensive coordinator Rod Dowhower scrapped that for a two-back, one tight-end look.

The Redskins opened the game in that alignment. But on their third series, they returned to Gibbs' set. The result: A 13-play, 80-yard drive that lasted 7:15 and ended with a 15-yard Rypien to receiver Ricky Sanders touchdown pass. Rookie running back Reggie Brooks gained 48 yards on this possession.

"We were concerned about Rod running the offense," receiver Art Monk said. "But he called a great game."

The Redskins played one. Dallas made sure it was Washington's night by losing four fumbles — five fewer than the Cowboys had the previous season.

And the Redskins' ground game humbled the Cowboys' defense, grinding out four drives of 65 yards or more.

"We were playing the world champs and it was a great showcase for us," Petitbon said. "We were very, very confident going in. We knew what [the Cowboys] wanted to try and do and we thought we'd be able to run the football on them. The game went about the way we thought it would go."

Only a short drive was needed for the Redskins' second score. Eilers recovered another fumbled punt — the ball had glanced off James Washington — for a first down at the Dallas 17.

Four plays later Brian Mitchell, making his first start at running back, swept in from the 1 with 40 seconds left in the first half. Nothing changed after halftime. On the Redskins' first second-half possession, a 78-yard drive, Mitchell's between-the-tackles runs led to a 1-yard scoring pass to tight end Ron Middleton and a 21-6 lead.

Dallas then rallied. The Cowboys needed just five plays to move 80 yards. Aikman completed four passes, the last of which covered 33 yards to Harper for the score.

Mitchell helped fuel Dallas' hopes on the ensuing kickoff. Already one of the game's best kick returners, Mitchell committed the ultimate gaffe. He fielded the kick and downed the ball. Problem was, Mitchell was on the 1-yard line.

"I felt two inches tall," Mitchell said.

But his mistake only set up a 99-yard drive, punctuated by Rypien's 15-yard touchdown pass to Monk. The 13-play, seven-minute march made it 28-13 and sucked the life out of Dallas.

Midway through that drive, Washington sensed Dallas had tired.

"You see them rotating defensive linemen in there because they're getting whipped and you've got the same group in," Redskins tackle Joe Jacoby said. "You know you've got them worn down."

All that remained was the final quarter, which proved to be a formality. No way would Washington lose this lead, not when the Redskins felt they had so much to prove. They showed to the 56,813 in attendance and to the nationally televised audience that Petitbon deserved this opportunity and that they could once more make a run at the Super Bowl.

"We weren't surprised we beat them, just how easy it was," Rypien recalled. "We didn't have any doubt that we were still a top team. That was one of the most satisfying games I've ever played in with the way the season had ended the year before."

Rypien completed 22-of-34 passes for 161 yards and three touchdowns; Mitchell rushed for 116 yards on 23 carries and scored the game's final touchdown on a 29-yard run late in the fourth quarter. And Elewonibi shut down Haley.

The Redskins rushed for 171 yards — 80 more than Dallas — and controlled the ball for 35:03. Brooks flashed his potential, gaining 53 yards on 11 carries.

"We ended up playing horrible defense," Johnson said. "We played poorly [as a team] and a lot of people said, 'Emmitt not being there didn't cause you to fumble the punt.' But I always attribute those things to not being focused and Emmitt not being there is why we weren't focused. And that's my fault. I should have had us more focused."

Smith's presence might not have mattered, according to Dallas' offensive coordinator Norv Turner.

"We just couldn't get the Redskins off the field," he said. "They just controlled the ball. The Redskins played so well, I felt the next time we played it would probably be for the division."

It wasn't.

The teams' fortunes changed rapidly after this game. Dallas lost the following week to visiting Buffalo, again minus Smith. After that game, Haley screamed in the locker room about not being able to win with a rookie running back as he slammed his helmet into the wall, cracking the wall and maybe the stalled negotiations.

Smith returned the following game. He helped Dallas finish the regular season 12-4 en route to its second straight Super Bowl victory.

Washington collapsed. Theories abound as to what happened, the simplest and most common being injuries. Only four players (cornerback Darrell Green, linebacker Kurt Gouveia, safety Brad Edwards and Middleton) started every game.

"We were hiring guys off the street," Jacoby said. "You're going to suffer through that and we did."

They lost six straight after beating Dallas.

"A lot of things happened that year," Redskins' tight ends coach Russ Grimm said. "It wasn't any reflection on Richie."

Still, by the following season, Rypien, Monk, Mann, Jacoby, Sanders, Bostic and running back Earnest Byner, among others, were gone. And Petitbon was fired, replaced by Turner.

The Redskins were about to embark on a serious facelift.

Said Mitchell, "We were at the end of an era."

REDSKINS 35, COWBOYS 16

	1	2	3	4	TOTAL
COWBOYS	6	0	7	3	16
REDSKINS	0	14	7	14	35

◆ FIRST QUARTER
D – Harper 80 pass from Aikman (kick failed), D 6-0
◆ SECOND QUARTER
W – Sanders 15 pass from Rypien (Lohmiller kick), W 7-6
W – Mitchell 1 run (Lohmiller kick), W 14-6
◆ THIRD QUARTER
W – Middleton 1 pass from Rypien (Lohmiller kick), W 21-6
D – Harper 33 pass from Aikman (Elliott kick), W 21-13
◆ FOURTH QUARTER
W – Monk 15 pass from Rypien (Lohmiller kick), W 28-13
D – Elliott 22 FG, W 28-16
W – Mitchell 29 run (Lohmiller kick), W 35-16

The Redskins bid farewell to RFK Stadium in style, helped in part by Brian Mitchell's long return.

Dec. 22, 1996

Farewell To RFK

Redskins 37, Cowboys 10

It was the king of all homecoming games, spurred by the return of Washington Redskins greats. The Redskins were leaving RFK Stadium after 36 seasons, and it was only fitting that the Cowboys be the opponent. Nothing would be sweeter for the Redskins — or their fans and alumni — than beating their old nemesis one last time.

After all, of the Redskins' 278 games in RFK since 1961, the NFC Championship victories in 1972 and 1982 over the Cowboys were considered the high marks of success. The first was the "Over The Hill Gang's" pinnacle, the second the start of coach Joe Gibbs' four conference titles. Nothing has ever measured up to them.

Fans arrived hours before the final game as the crisp holiday weather proved perfect for tailgate partying at 22nd and East Capitol Streets. Some fans had sat together for more than 30 years. Many fans married, raised families and had retired during those 36 seasons. There were even second generations of fans with sons and daughters succeeding the original season-ticket holders.

RFK seemed a second home, and no one was going to miss its going away party. Indeed, the need for remembrances was so passionate that game programs sold out nearly two hours before kickoff with scalpers offering the $5 souvenirs for $20.

"They became like brothers and sisters," said Jack Burt, a ticket holder since 1961, of his neighboring fans. "This is like home."

For weeks, it seemed the two teams would play for the NFC East title. A second-half collapse after a 7-1 start eliminated the Redskins (8-7) from the playoffs before the finale. The Cowboys (10-5) also lacked any incentive, having secured the division title the previous week.

Dallas coach Barry Switzer added fuel to the rivalry's fire in the previous days by calling the game a "bye week" for the Cowboys because it wouldn't affect their playoff positioning. Six starters — including running back Emmitt Smith and quarterback Troy Aikman — rested while five others were benched by the third quarter.

"Down the road, this game is like a molecule in the universe," Switzer said. "This game didn't mean anything. We did the right thing. No one likes to get beat, but we made that decision early in the week. Without Troy and Emmitt, we didn't expect that we would win the game, realistically. The Redskins are happy. Merry Christmas to them."

Smith had battled injuries all season, but he said, "I would have liked to have played because I scored my very first touchdown here [on Sept. 23, 1990] and I would have liked to have gotten one in the last game here. But I understand the big picture."

It didn't matter that the Cowboys lacked enthusiasm for the final game. The Redskins played on pure adrenaline. They wanted to make up for blowing their playoff berth with two overtime losses in recent weeks and three defeats to lowly Arizona and Tampa Bay. Washington didn't want to enter the long offseason with another loss ringing in its ears. Someone had to pay, and Dallas was the convenient opponent.

"It's Dallas. It's the last game at RFK," guard Bob Dahl said. "We won't have a problem being ready."

Redskins coach Norv Turner sensed something special during warmups. It was heartwarming to finally come home after playing three straight and four of five games on the road.

"I walked around the stadium and looked at all the former great players here," Turner said of the 32 former heroes who came to say goodbye. "I realized what it meant to be home, and that it was going to be a really special day."

The crowd of 56,454 — the 229th straight sellout — was still missing someone special, though. Redskins owner Jack Kent Cooke was vacant from his luxury suite for only the second time since 1979 because of illness. The 84-year-old owner would die from a heart attack nearly four months later, but he watched the game from his Washington home with general manager Charley Casserly. Of the near-billionaire's vast empire — from the Chrysler Building to the Los Angeles Daily News — nothing meant more to him than the Redskins.

"That's the one [game] I'll always remember," Casserly said. "I wanted to be there with him. I'd

105

been watching the games with the guy for eight years. He's your boss. You share the will to win. Something was missing if he wasn't there."

The Redskins quickly showed the Cowboys who would own the late afternoon game. On Dallas' second play, Washington linebackers Marvcus Patton and Rod Stephens burst through the line to tackle running back Sherman Williams for a 4-yard loss. The Cowboys would have to punt, and the Redskins followed with Scott Blanton's 55-yard field goal— third longest in team history — for a 3-0 lead with 6:23 remaining in the first quarter.

Blanton and Dallas' Chris Boniol traded field goals for a 6-3 Washington lead with 12:14 left in the first half. But that would be it for the visitors. Washington took a 16-3 halftime lead on running back Terry Allen's 1-yard touchdown run and Blanton's 18-yarder as time expired.

The halftime show may have lacked a homecom-ing queen, but it wasn't short on kings. Nearly three dozen of the Redskins' greatest players marched slowly onto the field. Linebacker Monte Coleman held his helmet high, his trademark of 16 seasons when playing a Redskins-record 216 games. Sonny Jurgensen started with a short jog before suddenly remembering these fans loved him as a paunchy passer so there was no reason to create the illusion that he was in great shape. Running back John Riggins donned a black leather outfit, showing time had not mellowed the rebel running back.

Defensive end Dexter Manley might have been the crowd favorite. The team all-time sack leader before drug problems shortened a possible Hall of Fame career and eventually sent him to prison, Manley ended a seven-year RFK absence only after coaxing by the Redskins. He was unsure whether the emotional event would prove overwhelming.

"I decided it would be selfish not to come," said Manley, who one day wants his ashes to be scattered at RFK. "I wanted to be here for the fans and the city. This place has meant so much for me."

The memorable players kept coming. It was Hog Heaven with Jeff Bostic, Russ Grimm, Joe Jacoby, Mark May, George Starke, Rick Walker, Fred Dean, Don Warren and Jim Lachey. Billy Kilmer, Larry Brown, Dave Butz, Gary Clark, Pat Fischer, Ken Houston, Sam Huff, Charles Mann, Ron McDole and Bobby Mitchell also lined the field. So did Art Monk, Mark Moseley, Mark Murphy, Mike Nelms, Brig Owens, Charley Taylor and Doug Williams. Darrell Green sprinted from the locker room as the only active player honored.

"A lot of memories will be lost," Kilmer said, "but they'll never die."

Many of the former players attended a reunion the preceding night at Fran O'Brien's Steak House, a fitting locale since O'Brien's five Redskins seasons included the final game at Griffith Stadium and the opener at D.C. Stadium that was later re-named RFK. For a few hours, the "Over the Hill Gang" conversed at the bar. Laughter filled the restaurant in the downtown hotel that ironically also housed the visiting Cowboys. Indeed, Switzer even stopped by for dinner.

"We all look the same as when we played," Kilmer said. "We're still not over

photo by Arnie Sachs/Consolidated News Pictures
Washington running back Terry Allen celebrates his third touchdown with the fans.

the hill yet. I don't think we've reached the summit yet."

Finally, the memorable players left the field. There were still 30 minutes more to play . . . and relish.

Blown leads characterized Washington's second-half breakdown and the Redskins wanted to avoid another. On their first possession, receiver Henry Ellard passed Hall of Famer Steve Largent for third in career receiving yardage with a 51-yarder to the Cowboys' 5. Allen would score on a 2-yard run, then celebrated his third touchdown by jumping into the stands.

"I just wanted to do something that hadn't been done," Allen said. "It was just impulsive. People were patting me on the back. They enjoyed it as much as I did."

The fans filled the stadium with a sea of yellow placards stating "Hail to the Redskins," replicating a 1991 moment during a playoff victory over Atlanta when thousands of yellow seat cushions filled the air during a playoff victory. It looked like something from a Hollywood movie. However, this kind of pure emotion can't be re-enacted . . . just enjoyed.

Allen later passed Riggins as the Redskins single-season rushing leader with 1,353 yards. Ellard, 35, became the first player to twice gain more than 1,000 yards receiving after age 34 with 1,014. Brian Mitchell joined superstars Gale Sayers and Jim Brown as the only players to lead the NFL in combined yardage three straight years with 2,001.

"It's a tremendous honor to be with Jim Brown and Gale Sayers," Mitchell said. "I didn't even know I had it until I was coming out [of the game]."

Allen's backup, Stephen Davis, later followed with a 4-yard touchdown for a 37-3 lead with 7:32 left. Cowboys running back Herschel Walker then scored the final touchdown at RFK with a 39-yard run, but it didn't matter. This game was over.

"As I walked off the field, it was a bittersweet moment," Turner said. "It was a great moment to beat the Cowboys, but there was frustration of what we didn't get done. Even when we were struggling, I thought we were going to be a playoff team. When we walked off the field, I saw we could have been one."

The fans were poised to celebrate. At first, a brave few trickled through the heavy security only to be caught. But it was only a temporary victory for law and order. Fans soon streamed past the guards, who quickly gave way to the flood of people that just wanted a souvenir.

In minutes, the field would look like a swarm of locusts had stripped it. End zone sections were gone. So were the yard lines. More than $100,000 in damage was inflicted on the grass field. The goal posts remained intact, but dozens of long-time ticket holders decided to take their seats with them. Even the players weren't safe from fan madness as helmets and game balls were stolen from the Redskins locker room.

"The party house was rocking, and there was anarchy out there," said Redskins guard Tre Johnson, who lost a football signed by teammates to the locker room thieves. "People were running on the field and just tearing up the place."

Washington quarterback Gus Frerotte was happy to depart RFK with a victory.

"This turned out great for the fans," he said. "They were super. I could imagine back in the old days and people chant 'We want Dallas!' how loud it must have been . . . To see Sonny and all the memories he had, I hope I can contribute a little bit of the memories the fans want."

Said 14-year cornerback Green: "With the exception of the Super Bowl, it doesn't get any better than this. You might have to ride all the way home with me before you could get an idea of what this day has meant to me . . . Nobody can leave here sad. We played every play hard. If I can't have what I want [a playoff berth], I'll take this."

The Redskins open the 1997 season with a 80,000-plus seat stadium in nearby Raljon, Md. It will be a stark contrast to the aging stadium that was a house of horrors for opponents, but one that Washingtonians will always love.

"It's the last time at RFK," Frerotte said, "and it will be sorely missed."

REDSKINS 37, COWBOYS 10				
COWBOYS	0	3	0	7	10
REDSKINS	3	13	7	14	37

◆ **FIRST QUARTER**
W - Blanton 45 FG, W 3-0

◆ **SECOND QUARTER**
W - Blanton 29 FG, W 6-0
D - Boniol 34 FG, W 6-3
W - Allen 1 run (Blanton kick), W 13-3
W - Blanton 18 FG, W 16-3

◆ **THIRD QUARTER**
W - Allen 2 run (Blanton kick), W 23-3

◆ **FOURTH QUARTER**
W - Allen 6 run (Blanton kick), W 30-3
W - Davis 4 run (Blanton kick), W 37-3
D - Walker 39 run (Boniol kick), W 37-10

About The Authors

Mickey Spagnola has covered the Dallas Cowboys since 1984. He's currently a columnist for The Insider, a fax publication covering the Cowboys, and a radio personality for The Ticket, KTCK-AM (1310) in Dallas. A graduate of the University of Missouri, Spagnola has won numerous writing awards during his 22-year sportswriting career. The South Chicago Heights, Ill. native currently resides in Carrollton, Texas with his wife Gail and daughter Erin.

John Keim is an award-winning sportswriter for the Journal newspapers in suburban Washington, D.C. for whom he has covered the Redskins since 1994. A co-author of "Hail to RFK! 36 Seasons of Redskins Memories," he has also written about the Redskins for Joe Theismann's Pro Football Yearbook and Redskin Review. The Ohio State graduate and Lakewood, Ohio native resides in Chantilly, Va. with his wife Kerry and son Matthew.

David Elfin has covered the Washington Redskins for six seasons for the Washington Times. Elfin, a native Washingtonian, is a graduate of the University of Pennsylvania. A co-author of "Hail to RFK! 36 Seasons of Redskins Memories," he has won numerous awards during his 15-year sportswriting career and serves on the board of directors of the Professional Football Writers of America. Elfin resides in Bethesda, Md. with his wife Loretta and daughters Julie and Amy.

Rick Snider covers the Washington Redskins for the Washington Times. An award-winning sportswriter for 19 years, the native Washingtonian has written six books, including "Hail to RFK! 36 Seasons of Redskins Memories" and a forthcoming "Health Secrets of the Rich and Famous." The University of Maryland graduate is the president of 21st Century Online Publishing, an Internet-based publishing company. Snider resides in Waldorf, Md. with his wife Lisa and daughters Megan and Katelyn.

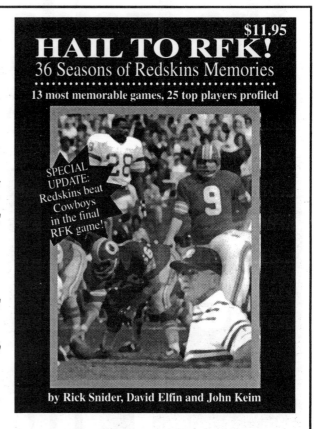
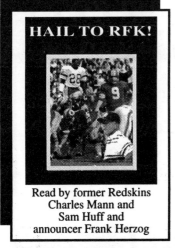

The Insider
America's Original SportsFAX

For the Ultimate Cowboy Fan

The Insider – Compelling. Insightful. Up-to-Date News and Commentaries.

Join the thousands of loyal Cowboy fans worldwide who read The Insider via fax or Email three times a week! Try it out for one month **FREE** and see why The Insider is best information source for the **Ultimate Cowboy Fan!**

Fax this form to (800) 226-6142
Or Email us at faxresc@onramp.net

Name (PLEASE PRINT CLEARLY)_____

Address_____

City_____ State_____ Zip_____

Phone Number (____) _____ Fax Number (____) _____

Email Address_____

Afterword

There's No Better Rivalry In The NFL

By Calvin Hill

Cowboys versus Indians! This is the Old West romanticized and revisited. East versus West. The rivalry between the Dallas Cowboys and Washington Redskins would have been special even if they had been ordinary NFL teams. However, there has been nothing ordinary about the Cowboys or Redskins over the past 30 years. Consider the coaches: Vince Lombardi, Tom Landry, George Allen, Joe Gibbs, Jimmy Johnson and Barry Switzer. Each coached teams to Super Bowls. All, with the exception of Allen, won a Super Bowl ring. And when it comes to Allen, he only has the best winning percentage of any NFL coach with more than 103 regular season victories. What prospective owner wouldn't love to hire one of these guys as his coach?

What about the players involved in this rivalry? How would you like to choose up sides? Pick from running backs such as Emmitt Smith, Tony Dorsett, Larry Brown and John Riggins. Would you line up with the Hogs — Joe Jacoby, Russ Grimm, Mark May and Jeff Bostic? Or would you rather have Erik Williams, Nate Newton, Larry Allen and Mark Tuinei? Why do I hear the names Rayfield Wright and Len Hauss? How about a foot race between Deion Sanders and Darrell Green? Could they beat Herschel Walker? And who would you pick, Roger Staubach, Troy Aikman, Sonny Jurgensen or Joe Theismann? Think about it.

When it comes to the owners — George Preston Marshall, Edward Bennett Williams, Clint Murchison, Jack Kent Cooke, Jerry Jones — each is unique as well as the owner of at least one Super Bowl ring. (By the way, why do

Redskins owners use three names and Cowboys owners only two?)

Allow me to advance this hypothesis: The Cowboys versus Redskins rivalry was at full throttle during the early 1970s when televised football experienced an explosion. How many times were the matchups between Allen's Redskins and Landry's Cowboys nationally televised? Remember Ken Houston's last-second, goal-line tackle of Walt Garrison on Monday night? Clint Longley's last-second "mad bomb" to Drew Pearson on Thanksgiving Day? Tex Schramm insisting that Mark Moseley's kicking shoe was illegal?

This rivalry helped to make the NFL the media entertainment giant it is today. It is a rivalry usually loaded with playoff or championship game implications. The Cowboys and Redskins have played in 13 Super Bowls, combining to win eight.

Please consider this irony: I personally know a guy who had become the Cowboys' first 1,000-yard rusher in a game against the Redskins (1972) and who scored the go-ahead touchdown for Washington in its first victory at Texas Stadium (1976). Guess who?

Finally, isn't it interesting that the coach who had everybody in Washington excited in 1997 was the former Dallas offensive coordinator whose schemes spurred the Cowboys to two Super Bowls in the 1990s? The Redskins and Cowboys. How their successes and failures seem so intertwined.

Calvin Hill was a running back with Dallas from 1969-74 and with Washington from 1976-77. Hill is currently a consultant to the Cowboys for player assistance and development.